Curiosity.

2019

The Cura Convergence

Healing Through Science and Spirit

Dr. Jill Strom

BALBOA.
PRESS

A DIVISION OF HAY HOUSE

www.curaintegrative.com

Art & Photography Credits
Joshua Van Shipley Design www.shipleydesign.com
Leeanne Seaver Creative www.seavercreative.com

Book Design
Joshua Van Shipley www.shipleydesign.com

Author photo by Seaver Creative

Balboa Press books may be ordered through booksellers or by contacting:

Balboa Press
A Division of Hay House
1663 Liberty Drive
Bloomington, IN 47403
www.balboapress.com
1 (877) 407-4847

Because of the dynamic nature of the Internet, any web addresses or links contained in this book may have changed since publication and may no longer be valid. The views expressed in this work are solely those of the author and do not necessarily reflect the views of the publisher, and the publisher hereby disclaims any responsibility for them.

The author of this book does not dispense medical advice or prescribe the use of any technique as a form of treatment for physical, emotional, or medical problems without the advice of a physician, either directly or indirectly. The intent of the author is only to offer information of a general nature to help you in your quest for emotional and spiritual well-being. In the event you use any of the information in this book for yourself, which is your constitutional right, the author and the publisher assume no responsibility for your actions.

Any people depicted in stock imagery provided by Thinkstock are models, and such images are being used for illustrative purposes only. Certain stock imagery © Thinkstock.

Print information available on the last page.

ISBN: 978-1-5043-8165-9 (sc)
ISBN: 978-1-5043-8166-6 (hc)
ISBN: 978-1-5043-8176-5 (e)

Library of Congress Control Number: 2017907378

Balboa Press rev. date: 10/25/2017

 Table of Contents

Foreword

When we ponder the meaning of health, we may reference the definition by the World Health Organization: "a state of complete physical, mental, and social well-being" or "a state of balance, and equilibrium that an individual has established within oneself and with the environment." We may go on to explore other definitions for clarity such as this one from The Free Dictionary which says health is "a relative state in which one is able to function well physically, mentally, socially, and spiritually in order to express the full range of one's unique possibilities within the environment in which one is living." These definitions may still fall short; we may not have words to express it, but we "know it when I see it" intuitively.

However it is defined, the bigger question is how do we achieve this state of balance—this equilibrium of mind, body, and spirit? In conventional Western medicine, technical and scientific advancements have brought about techniques and medicines to "fix" the physical body—in some ways quite miraculously. Conventional medicine, however, often doesn't address the emotional/mental component of health (patients are referred to psychologists or social workers) or the spiritual (patients are encouraged to work with their clergy). In this current Western model, physicians often don't have the training nor the time to really know their patients who come to them for healing.

As a child growing up in the Midwest, I very much wanted to be a healer. In the 1950s and 1960s, for girls that meant becoming a nurse—which I did in the 1970s. During my formative years, I was blessed to be raised in a church that fostered strong spiritual connections with God, that believed in the worth of all persons, and used "laying on of hands" for healing. I never doubted there would be life after death. In my faith tradition and in my work, I saw healing take place in many situations, even in death. Over time I wanted to know more, understand more, and do more, so I decided to enter medical school. As I took classes to prepare for entry, I recognized the coursework was very reductionistic—based on biology/physical body and the science of nature, not the wonder of nature. At times, these teachings often conflicted with what I knew intuitively and spiritually, and made me question the body-soul connection. I really struggled when my beloved grandmother died in the midst of this training—was that the end for her, for our relationship? One day in my college physics class, we were learning the basic laws of nature—specifically the law that states that energy can neither be created nor destroyed. Rather, it transforms from one form to another. This was an epiphany for me recognizing that biology and energy do come together, that science and spirituality meet—that these were not exclusive of each other, but inclusive and part of the whole. This validated the physical/mental/emotional/spiritual nature of all beings in a wholeness that cannot and should not be separated.

This idea of wholeness/connectedness—that all is tied together energetically—has remained with me ever since, even as I practice medicine today. My training in Integrative Medicine at the Arizona Center in Integrative Medicine further bound these concepts as we learned of the energetic/healing nature of foods, herbs, homeopathy, healthy relationships, acupuncture, mind-body therapies, healthy lifestyles, osteopathy, energy medicine, prayer, and more. What we learned, and what I continue to believe, is that there are many paths to healing including surgery and medicines. As we are all unique individuals, so, too, should each person's approach be to their own healing. This is not at "one-size-fits-all" concept, as is frequently seen in conventional Western medicine, but the ultimate form of "individualized medicine." There is plenty of room in healing for the *both/and* union of Eastern and Western medicine. Fortunately, there is more evidence being published each day in medical journals showing the efficacy of integrative medicine to help those that still question.

Dr. Jill Strom has beautifully and eloquently brought the concepts of wholeness—**Cura**—together in this book. She explains the convergence of energy, biology, and spirituality through the science known to us today. These concepts support why we need to integrate the wisdom and knowledge of Eastern medicine and other traditional healing practices into our Western medical model to bring about the profound healing we all seek and deserve. She further helps us understand our personal role in creating our own healing path through our conscious choices. **Cura** gently guides us through the process of letting go of that which does not serve us well and accepting the natural flow of life with its beginnings and endings. Dr. Jill is a true healer and now shares her wisdom to unite us in this **Cura Convergence**.

Joy A. Weydert, MD, FAAP
Professor, Integrative Medicine and Pediatrics
University of Kansas Health System

# How to Read Cura

This book comes to those who can conceive that science and spirituality aren't mutually exclusive. If you have come to the point in your journey where you know there is something more—and that "something" is the key to everything—this book is for you.

If you are a healer, if you need healing, if you want to live more consciously and intentionally as a human being engaged in your own or another's healing process, this book is for you. The chapters scaffold with meaning—watch for terms that are in bold print. They are establishing a context for the Cura Healing Convergence chart (Figure 5.1 in Chapter Five) that depicts the multidimensional relationship of science and spirit that is at the heart of all healing.

Everything in the universe exists in an ever-changing, ever-transforming cycle. While the content of this book is stamped in a linear fashion, it breathes and grows. It is important to allow space for an ever-expanding perspective and consciousness that is yet to be known.

"Our theories determine what we measure," Einstein once said. The idea of actually integrating Eastern and Western medicine has rarely been considered, even theoretically, so the body of evidence measuring its connectedness and effectiveness doesn't fully exist in an academic sense.

It is time for both schools to blend their approaches to medicine and healing, philosophically and functionally. The body of evidence we seek is our own; each one of us individually and all of us collectively. Every effort we make to discover the Cura—true healing—will reveal that this is an integrative process of science and spirit.

Jill M. Strom

Preface

The Book of Joan

The beginning of one thing is always the ending of something else, even if those events take time to unfold.

My life began in a hospital room with my mother on March 14th. Hers ended exactly 28 years later in 2008, to the day, but under very different circumstances. It is the similarity that strikes me. A hospital room. Quiet noises of people and machines, loved ones gathered. My mother cradling me when I entered this world . . . me holding her in my arms as she left it.

The world stops when such profound things are happening. These are moments of complete presence: birth and death. Death and birth. The beginning of something . . . the end of something.

After my mother died, the world stopped for many of us. Over a thousand people came to pay respects at her visitation, and many more were with us in spirit for her memorial service that followed. We were enveloped with loving support. Happiness and sorrow curl into the yin and yang of that day. I am reminded of beginnings and endings, healing and disease, life and death . . . of the delicate balance between honoring a life and mourning a death, between creation and destruction.

My mother, Joan Snider Strom Millard, taught my brothers and me, and everyone who knew her, to live our passion: to recognize our purpose and know it as a calling. Hers was to be a visionary and healer in the spiritual sense. She was dynamic, spirit-led, and stubborn. She was a pastor, a leader, and a matriarch.

Our mother felt a profound sense of purpose in ministering to others, and committed her life to her church. There were strong family values embodied in that commitment—we were all raised to be of service to others. You worked hard and did anything that was asked of you—especially if it was church-related.

These are admirable qualities, and not uncommon during my mother's era, particularly amongst the devout. However, the unintended consequence of such selflessness was to grow up without a strong sense of one's self. For my mother and her siblings, it was understood that the needs of others were always more important than their own. This may be the stuff of great humanitarians, but it can also stymie self-awareness and self-care. If you never focus on your own feelings, you can end up not knowing how you really feel. How do you gain a sense of self if you are unaware of your own feelings? What happens when you live a life that is exemplary of what others expect of you, but is devoid of your own authentic presence in some very important ways?

I don't know if my mother would characterize her life that way, but I do know that getting cancer prompted levels of self-discovery that Joan had never given herself the time to indulge. It wasn't until she got sick that my mother had the compulsion to feel her own vulnerability that had lived for years unacknowledged behind her drive and focus on others.

Cancer prompted Joan (my mother) to learn about herself for her own sake. She began to see spirituality on a infinite scale: not just in the lectionaries and church pews, but in the silence of the internal landscape of her individual relationship with her God. She found the courage to confront the emotional scars of abandonment and a traumatic divorce from my dad, the loneliness and anxiety of single parenting, and, ultimately, the philosophical dismissal of her truth by the beloved institution of the church to which she had dedicated her life.

Given our religious orientation, most of the family viewed Joan's cancer from a spiritual vantage point—what could we learn from this? What would true healing look like?

Over the course of six years in treatment, Mom had three remissions and vast personal and spiritual awakenings. She devoted herself to directing Camp Quality, a cancer camp for kids, and continued as pastor at her church. Long stretches of relative "normal" would be punctuated by bad news from a follow-up test. Somehow Mom would keep all the plates spinning for everybody while tending to herself as holistically as possible. Joan watched her younger sister, Jane Snider Shipley, devote herself to integrative healing to overcome a condition that doctors said would make her wheelchair-bound. That was how my mom wanted to approach her own healing journey.

> **Jesus said the Kingdom of God is at hand. Maybe it has existed for all these 2000 years for anyone who chose to see it and engage in the reality. Maybe our call hasn't been so much to build it, but rather to recognize it, and to act with integrity consistent with the Kingdom of God in all our relationships. When we see the Kingdom already in our**

midst, it can create an empowerment in our living, our ministry, and our response in the world. It calls for participation, for it is when energy meets up with other energy that new possibilities are created. There is power in participation and our thoughts create before form is given. Awakening to these concepts is what may in fact allow us to finally respond to the call of being the Kingdom of God on earth, for we will finally understand how! The Quantum Kingdom of God is when we see ourselves reflecting that vision and when we let it define everything we do. Then, and only then, we create Heaven on Earth!

– Joan Snider Strom Millard

Mom's younger sister, Jane, walked her own path from the straight and narrow confines of their childhood and "churchhood" until it crippled her, literally. There were days when she could barely get out of bed. She was only in her 30s when she was diagnosed with a condition that atrophied her lower extremities to the point where doctors told her she would likely never walk again. My aunt's healing journey taught me first-hand that "our biography becomes our biology," as author and medical intuitive Caroline Myss put it. After many unsuccessful attempts at healing via traditional medical interventions, Jane decided to take a completely different, holistic tact. The message my aunt internalized growing up was that there was only one way to walk "the old, old path" but living her own life authentically took her far beyond it. She had to break free of the rigidity that bound her and find her own way through claiming her body and her spirit. When she did, Jane healed.

Jane's healing stemmed from a conscious, intentional, natural approach which made the most sense to my mom, who then committed herself to the same healing process. My mom rejected the idea that the manifestations of her woundedness could simply be cut out of her in a literal sense. Instead, Mom chose to focus on healing the cause—not just the symptoms of her disease.

Joan engaged in a number of healing modalities, went on a sabbatical, and connected to her Native American roots. She devoured books by Caroline Myss, Bruce Lipton, and Candace Pert. She allowed her body to sweat every day, alkalized her diet, drank pH-balanced "love and gratitude" water. Daily prayer ties, healing and sweat lodges, walking meditations and journaling became routine. The house would smell of sage and sweetgrass. This opened her ability to connect to the point where she would gain ground and we would get an "all clear" remission report. A typical driver-personality, once she went into remission, she would vigorously return to a full roster of obligations, and the old pattern of her life repeated. To anyone who needed it, she gave her Lifeforce, exhausting herself with the effort. A year later, the cancer returned.

We coped. Our daily walks were replaced by card games during chemo. Patches of her hair were falling out onto her pillow. A port was placed in her chest where my head used to nestle.

She still traveled to see her acupuncturist, still continued to alkalize her diet. She still tried to balance various modalities of healing. Her second regression occurred within the year, and she was back to her daily walking trails.

After my mom's regression, I stepped into my calling. I'd seen Jane stand up and walk. Mom's remission was achieved holistically. I was ready. I began studying with Master Chen to become an acupuncturist, and I enrolled at Cleveland Chiropractic College. In 2010, I passed the national boards and received my Doctor of Chiropractic Medicine and also became a Fellow with the Acupuncture Society of America.

I had a strong sense of the efficacy of those approaches and wanted to study them more thoroughly. We were willing to utilize all holistic measures to help restore her health. But then we watched her regress again. We shifted again into Western medicine, which bought us more time—we would do anything for more time. Mom regressed until nothing from Western or Eastern medicine could help us. We were losing her.

Since he was a little boy, my older brother Jeremy also wanted to be a doctor. His passion led him along a more traditional path. Today he is a Pulmonary and Critical Care Physician. Dr. Jeremy Strom saves lives with his expertise in Western medicine. He is there at the most critical and intense moments for families. And he shows up with loving presence, a sharp mind, and the clinical expertise that reassures even the most anxious patients.

As Jeremy and I continue to study and practice medicine, our sometimes-polarized views typify our family of origin. We both bring a different kind of expertise but have the same passion and goal. Our calling is different by divine design. We approach our healing work with unique skill sets from different perspectives in various roles ranging from medicine to ministry, or both. Jeremy and I have been—sometimes lovingly, sometimes not—at the exact opposite ends of the spectrum: traditionalist and non-conformist; masculine versus feminine; Western versus Eastern. We cover a continuum, and the beautiful part of a continuum is that there is always middle ground. There is always a point where the extremes come together—a point of connection. I know I speak for both of us when I say that the connected, grounded place is our mother's energy inside and around us.

Jeremy was in medical school during Mom's illness, and he watched her decision-making in horror. He had access to cutting edge research and medical experts, so he left no stone unturned in finding out all the latest advancements on breast cancer treatment. He knew Mom's diagnosis, *intraductal carcinoma*, was ninety-eight percent curable when removed early. Her choice not to do so made him desperate and angry.

Jeremy's Story

> When it came to Mom and her diagnosis, I was the outlier of the family. Everybody was on board with her spiritual journey, but I wanted to help my mom the way I knew how—the proven way. I was just going into medical school, but I stopped and spent all my time researching Mom's breast cancer. I sent it all to her, the latest and best, but she said no. She could be incredibly stubborn. We spent the next few years discussing all this, and from my perspective, she didn't pursue Western medicine until it was later than it needed to be. She pursued acupuncture, meditation, spiritual healing, and water therapy. By the time I'd convinced her to use the resources of Western medicine, it had spread. We started chemo shortly thereafter.

It was December 2007. I was working for the nephrologist at my training facility and I got a call from saying, "Your mom is here. She's got a lesion in her brain." I remember going straight to the hospital, trying to help direct the next steps in her care. In typical dispassionate discussions, the doctor said, "Joan, do you want chest compressions or shocks?" She replied, "No." We all said that is not happening! We pushed her into having surgery—I feel like I made her have the tumors removed. So she did. Then three months later, it had metastasized to a location under the brainstem. If you leave it there, it pinches off connection to the brain. The surgery can also cause enough swelling to close everything down . . . so you're damned if you do, damned if you don't. The cancer had scattered throughout her whole body. She shifted to palliative care then, and passed away on March 14th. It was Jill's birthday.

– Jeremy Strom, MD

Jeremy was inconsolable. The last week of Joan's life, he was in her hospital room daily, pacing, crazy with grief because he couldn't bring her back and he couldn't reach her. By mid-week Mom was drifting in and out. Jeremy and I were sitting beside her when she commented, "Tomorrow at 2:00 pm." I knew exactly what she meant. I told my Aunt Jane to gather the family. At 1:50 pm the next afternoon, March 13th, Mom was sitting there listening to music, bobbing her head in her Mickey Mouse cap, when she said to no one in particular, "I think I'm going to make that two o'clock." A few minutes later, she said, "Ohhh, we're not in Kansas anymore," and closed her eyes. My step-dad Ron, her siblings, parents, and all of us kids were

there in the room. We were all so stunned. We just watched her as she fell asleep so peacefully.

Mom only woke up one more time, just after midnight in the wee hours of March 14th. She gasped and called my name. I quietly crawled into bed with her, and with silent tears streaming down my face, I talked to her, stroked her skin, and held her. Later in the morning, she passed.

As a doctor, what I know regarding the relationship between illness and wellness has been uniquely cultivated and enlightened by that experience. I have come to realize that my mother gave me a great gift in sharing intimately her illness, her healing, and her dying. That I can speak of her passing as a gift and lesson is one of the reasons I feel called to write this book—as a daughter and a healer. To understand how she truly healed even though she passed on is to comprehend the multidimensionality of wellness—to redefine healing and to see it differently than we normally view such things in this culture. We don't have a very complete lexicon for this in our traditional medical practice, but we need one.

One of the last things my mom said to my brother and me was, "You two are supposed to work together, in balance, to blend medicine and healing." At the time, Jeremy and I were suffering the pain of losing her, especially because we both knew it might have been avoided. I don't know how her words ever found a way to plant themselves in our broken hearts. But grieving, then learning how to live without her, and then realizing how much we needed each other gave us cause to reflect and reconnect. My brother and I found the seed of the idea she had rooted deeply in our sense of purpose. It was very much alive and it wanted to grow.

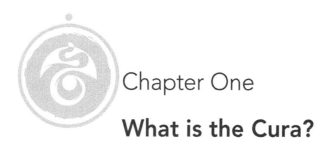

Chapter One

What is the Cura?

Cura in Latin means *the cure*—restoring the body, mind, and spirit to health. Restoring health can be a simple process, but usually the more complicated the cause, the more complex the cure. Science tries to impose objectivity over healing while each one of us lives a life of subjectivity. We always ponder: Do we inherit our health? Has our lifestyle made us sick? Why do some of us get well while others don't? Most important: how can we heal and stay well?

Our body wants to heal. It has the capacity to restore itself to stasis—the state of health and wellness. In a dynamic, multidimensional convergence of energy, biology, and spirituality, the true Cura is working towards this end at every moment in every way. When we understand the way of restoration and healing, then we understand the essence of Cura.

It's not magic, it's science. It's not just science, it's miraculous. What if we knew how to engage the miraculous because we understood it scientifically?

Actually, the science behind explanations of energy began to emerge as early as 1900 in the west, although it had been a traditional practice in China for over two thousand years. What was being discovered by astrophysicists would take decades to apply to the field of medicine. It would take much longer for

Quantum physics to be understood as a kind of lexicon for Chinese medicine. Merging Eastern and Western medicine Is the next frontier. The future of medicine depends on this kind of thinking: the Cura is merging and converging the things that need to work together for healing.

> **What we're learning is a new kind of science. It's an inner science that marries the subjective and the objective, in which you become familiar with the workings of your own body. That doesn't mean that you could write a scientific treatise about it. What it means is that you'll live more intelligently. You'll make decisions that are more apt to bring you in touch with the way things work for you in the world. – Jon Kabat-Zinn**[1]

The Cura Convergence is the threshold where science and spirit merge in the restoration of healing and wholeness. This point of convergence is where the construction or deconstruction of health and wellness happens, and where true healing must focus. At the quantum level where formlessness manifests into form, there is Divinity—by whatever name—that permeates every aspect of a profoundly complex and beautiful process.

As I watch my patients heal in ways that defy their diagnosis, I feel compelled to share that this new frontier is a miraculous place. There is no doubt that all healing is happening here, even if we don't always recognize the efficacy of it or how to get here intentionally.

All over the world, there are medical establishments, offices, and centers where patients search for healers who have responded to a sense of calling to serve their communities as wellness and health care professionals. Doctors, nurses, and practitioners of every healing modality from Western or Eastern approaches are motivated by a love of people and an instinctive desire to end suffering. Yet, they face barriers to act on those good intentions.

There is a crisis within the health care system today. More specifically, a conflict between health care modalities, techniques, and professionals—a tension that has been reinforced with years of history. In recent decades, this debate has focused on the real and perceived differences between Eastern and Western healing.

Within the last few years, science has made enormous strides in understanding the universe and providing state-of-the-art medicine and care. And yet, even as science is making advancements with technology and medicine, we are losing ground between doctors and patients. Individualized therapies, direct communication, and continuity of care are outmoded in favor of specialization. Patients must seek advice from multiple doctors, each with a different focus, and most of whom do not communicate with one another. The patient is left to decide which opinion, medication, or treatment to follow in order to maintain or regain their health.

It will be detrimental to society if the health care system continues in this manner. Medical specialization takes an expert but myopic view. What we have gained with professionals who have a distinctive expertise has been critically important in diagnostics, but this often costs us the bigger picture. Instead of looking at the dimensionality of an individual, it breaks up the body into organ system functions: digestive, immune, pulmonary, cardiovascular, etc.

While it is imperative to understand how the physiology of each organ system functions, we do ourselves a disservice when we base healing on the notion that these systems work separate and distinct from each other. The body utilizes and relies on all aspects of its being in order to heal and function. The body is synergistic and integrated. It is best understood from both Western and Eastern perspectives. Good medicine and effective healing must be as well.

The healing of mind, body, and spirit requires a multidimensional approach. In an age of increasingly detached doctoring in silos of unshared information, the holistic relationship between mind, body, and spirit is often overlooked. Therefore, a lot of healing potential gets missed. How did these paths diverge so distinctly? You'd have to go back only a few hundred years to find the point of departure.

Throughout human history, healers used both *Cataphatic* knowledge and *Apophatic* wisdom to treat the sick. Cataphatic knowledge is associated with left-brain, analytical thinking: things that are proven, deducible, objective, predictable, measurable, palpable, and "scientific." Every civilization recognized healers who were trained in this tradition—it isn't new. Mummified skeletons showed evidence that the first primitive brain surgery was performed over two thousand years ago in ancient Egypt. That emerging knowledge was added to ancient Apophatic wisdom—the kind that draws from the right-brain. It uses homeopathic, herbal medicine, intuition, tradition, dreams, signs, symbolic sight, animism, and many other intangible but important ways of knowing something.

Both approaches were recognized, respected, complementary, and integrated.

Whatever balance had worked for centuries began to shift in the early 17th century. The father of modern philosophy, Rene Descartes, posited that man consisted of two things: mind (his consciousness and spirit) and matter (his physical form). Referred to as *Cartesian Dualism*, this view that the body and mind are two distinct and disintegrated things relegated consciousness and spirit to religion and the church; the body and anything material or measurable to science. These distinctions mark the rise of scientific, rational Cataphatic thought, and the decline and departure from intuitive Apophatic wisdom.

For thousands of years, in every society, the healers—medicine men and women, the crones and *Curanderas*—had been revered and respected for their Apophatic traditions. But the wisdom of these healers, oracles, seers, diviners, crones, medicine men, and wise women was discredited and even outlawed as the church dispassionately removed all threats to its authority. In the secular world, knowing something for an evidenced-based fact became the only acceptable mode of thinking as science began to explain the forces that, until then, had been considered metaphysical.

In 1687, Sir Isaac Newton published his *Laws of Motion* and with it created a model of the universe that was solely defined in terms of matter. With our understanding of how gravity worked came the growing expectation that everything must have a scientific explanation—a cause to every effect. Newtonian Physics became the law of the land and the advancements of civilization made great strides.

Science made forays into explaining life itself in evolutionary terms. Early in the 19th century, Jean Baptiste Lamarck theorized that organisms evolved by gaining (or losing) a function or behavior that was crucial to their survival in a given environment. That characteristic was then passed along in the DNA to their offspring genetically. Over time, a "transmutation of the species" happened and that's how evolution worked according to Lamarckism.

In 1859, Charles Darwin's *Origin of Species* explained evolution as a process of natural selection. Creationism aside, Darwin's theory was widely accepted. Lamarckism went the way of the flat-earth theory until, relatively recently, the Neo-Lamarckism movement regained ground with evidence that Darwin and Lamarck might both be right.[2]

Revisiting Lamarck is no minor footnote in understanding the mind-body connection in our health. "Lamarck is being rehabilitated into the new Darwin," writes Pulitzer Prize-winning science writer Siddhartha Mukherjee.[3] Research is proving that environmental conditions, both externally and internally, have an impact on our genetics, or more specifically our *epigenetics*.

*Epi*genetics (from the Greek "epi"—*above*) is a term coined by Conrad Waddington, an English embryologist, back in the 1940s. The epigenome is a set of protein structures that surround our DNA. These proteins are responsible for signaling and allowing specific genes to be regulated up or down. Waddington's theory was that "cells acquire their identities just as humans do—by letting nurture (environmental signals) modify nature (genes)," according to Mukherjee. Today, science is discovering that "the genome is not a passive blueprint: the selective activation or repression of genes allows an individual cell to acquire its identity and to perform its function."[4]

The takeaway: whatever your DNA inheritance dealt, your genetic hand is not the only game in process. Every minute of every day, the variables of your life are at play through the epigenetics affecting your physical and mental health. Environmental factors are not limited to your physical setting. Our diet and lifestyle, our thoughts and the emotional climate within and around us—how we think and feel—influence our epigenetics. How we interpret that input emotionally is conveyed via neuropeptides that attach to receptor sites in every cell throughout our body. "The receptor is the interface where behavior meets biochemistry," according to Candace Pert, PhD, the award-winning research scientist and author who discovered endorphins.[5]

Emerging science is proving and affirming the profound influence of our mind and mental state over the health of our body—right down to our evolving genetic code.

Over the last 300 years, science has explored the great mystery of our still-evolving creation. Yet scientific influence on medicine has been limited by the centuries-old division between science and religion. When our minds isolate the universe by Newtonian Physics, anything that lies beyond the law of matter is typically discredited or deemed irrelevant. In so doing, we limit the great mystery and unfolding knowledge of the expansive quantum universe never imagined by Sir Isaac Newton. Emerging science serves to remind us that there is always more to know. What was once accepted as fact—the law of the land—falls away as greater understandings evolve.

Not understanding or lacking experience or expertise with something at the Cataphatic or Apophatic level does not render that theory, practice, belief, or tradition null, void or worthless. Our knowledge and our wisdom are also evolving. Ironically, that evolution is influenced by many variables including our own consciousness, whether we are aware it or not. Finding the Cura is an exploration beyond the known into the mystery of the universe. This holistic process is true for humanity collectively, and for each of us individually—both holograph and holon.

Holistic medicine integrates diverse modalities in the process of treating and healing each patient across the spectrum of mind, body, and spirit. Like the confluence of rivers, such expansiveness enables greater possibilities to flow together to deliver more results by working with the natural order of the body. Our bodies are designed to heal themselves. Yes, we may need varying degrees of help in that process, and when Western and Eastern medicines are joined effectively, the best potential for healing is created.

For genuine healing to occur, hearts and minds must be open to a self-awareness of the cause and effect of our lives and lifestyles on our health. Healing can occur on different levels, but true healing occurs when it happens in an integrated fashion, holistically—on all levels: energetically, biologically, and spiritually.

Turning to others for help in healing is the nature of humanity. Always in our midst are those who are uniquely gifted as healers. Most people can readily name whom they turn to in times of heartache or suffering. When it comes to illness in the physical form, most of us have a doctor, a specialist, or even multiple health care professionals who guide us and watch over our care.

> **Sometimes "good medicine" doesn't come in the form of a pill or test. It comes in the form of a person. A person who is willing to go beyond the limits of their technical**

expertise and professional requirements. People who, at their core, seek to understand and accept all that come along their path. These are the ones who never miss a chance for improvement or healing.
– Jeremy Strom, MD

Practitioners are here to help people heal. This is all any kind of healer can do—help a person in his or her process of healing. Every one of us must engage in our own dynamic, dimensional process with every resource available to us.

The dynamic between traditional and "alternative" medicine needs healing. We are at a pivotal point in human history where the resources of Eastern and Western medicine, of Apophatic and Cataphatic knowing, and of our own innate, individual role in the process must be united respectfully and reverently to cure ourselves and help heal this world.

Chapter Two

Embodiment: How Energy Becomes You

> You may consider yourself an individual, but as a cell biologist, I can tell you that you are in truth a cooperative community of approximately fifty trillion single-celled citizens. – Bruce Lipton

Form.

The human form, the body.

Your body is an embodiment of energy manifesting into trillions of cells, each with unique purpose and highly specialized variability. All are a part of you, a unique individual who is also part of humanity as a whole.

Scientifically speaking, aren't we divinely made? Across space and time, our bodies were created or they evolved into the complex dynamics of their function, whether by an act of God or science. Or both/and.

In his book, *The World as I See It*, Albert Einstein articulated his personal belief that science and God are not mutually exclusive, but part of what he termed <u>Universal Intelligence</u>. "Human intelligence is a small but elegant expression of this larger intelligence and has much to learn from it."[6]

Indeed, humans have been learning intently. How our bodies work, and what to do if they're not working well, has been a common concern since the dawn of human existence. If we're paying attention, our bodies will tell us what they do (and don't) need. Fortunately, **Universal Intelligence** has imbued us with an autonomic operating system that works whether we're listening or not. "The harmony of natural law reveals an intelligence of such superiority that, compared with it, all the systematic thinking and acting of human beings is an utterly insignificant reflection," Einstein stated.

Where does that natural law come from? Can we ever really know? Whatever the answer may be, there is something innate within human beings that must ask where and why and how life works.

This quest led Newtonian Science to beget Biology, the formal study of Life's natural laws, along with Physiology—how our bodily functions work together—as modern sciences in the 17th century. During that era, modern medicine emerged, diverging from its Apophatic roots. In the 20th Century, Quantum Physics provided a new perspective on biological and physiological phenomena at the smallest quantifiable level.

At the quantum level, Universal Intelligence prompts sub-atomic potential into atoms and mass—into something atomic—kinetic, real, physical, and quantifiable. Something in the natural order of things generates this transmutation of energy into mass—from our bodies to our bodily functions to everything else that runs on energy—but how and why?

Medicine itself would like to answer that question, but its grounding in Newtonian Science presents serious challenges and limitations.

The understanding of energy and its working at the level of subatomic particles cannot be predicted by Newtonian Physics. Early scientists tried to correlate energy and frequency with a formula that would be known as Planck's constant. In 1900, theoretical physicist Max Planck developed this logarithm to quanticize light and matter. It proved unreliable as a constant when early physicists noted inconsistencies in function, wavelength, momentum, and position once a particle got below a certain size. Indeed, classical physics couldn't explain the variability of energy outside the Newtonian context.

Ultimately, this dilemma led to Planck's development of quantum theory—the origins of the field of Quantum Physics. William Nelson, author of *Towards a Bio-Quantum Matrix*, wrote, "If the dimensions fall underneath Planck's constant, then we will need a quantic understanding in order to surmise what the possibilities are in the system."[7]

Given that Newtonian laws can't inform the process during which energy embodies, then it follows that traditional medicine, based on Newtonian Laws, has a limited view when it comes to addressing the complicated origins of disease in its energetic form. As Nelson put it, "Modern medicine must walk the Planck's constant."

> **Einstein revealed that we do not live in a universe with discrete, physical objects separated by dead space. The Universe is one indivisible, dynamic whole in which energy and matter are so deeply entangled it is impossible to consider them as independent elements. – Bruce H. Lipton**

Everything looks different from a quantic perspective.

Energy slowing down enough to become a particle in dimensional existence is the point referred to as *rest mass energy*. It is literally mass, at rest; no wavelength, no vibration. This is the most fundamental, quantifiable amount of energy that is needed to create a particle.[8] Rest mass energy crosses the **Line of Transmutation** from formlessness into form when the vibration of energy shifts from wave to particle. (See Figure 2.1) It manifests as matter—a quantifiable amount of physical matter. So, the subatomic particles now possess new atomic properties on the physical plain as well as their energetic properties—they are both potential and kinetic; again—*both/and*.

Subatomic particles form to create **atoms**. Atoms are comprised of 99.9% intangible empty space: energy and frequency. What remains is less than one percent made up of matter—or more specifically, the potential to become matter.[9]

For molecular biologist Bruce Lipton, this discovery was a complete game changer. "At the atomic level, matter does not even exist with certainty; it only exists as a tendency to exist. All my certitudes about biology and physics were shattered."[10]

In terms of our own body's "creation story" or biological incarnation, this begins with procreation—a particularly powerful example of transmutation. Every step of the process is fueled by energy as an electromagnetic force prompting growth (or evolution), dividing cells again and again to form increasingly complex levels of organization.

Atoms bond to become molecules.

Molecules link to create a chemical.

Chemicals organize to form cells.

Cells join to create tissues.

Tissues combine to form **organs**.

Organs develop into **organ systems.**

Organ systems function together to regulate the balance and homeostasis of the human body: our operating system. While the organ systems are classified separately in terms of cell development and function, they are organized at a higher level in terms of human physiology. With each increasing level of organization, there is a greater degree or level of complexity.

Organ systems join to create an organism—and there you are, the human form.

You.

You are the **embodiment** of matter. You have incarnated.

You matter.

Figure 2.1 depicts the levels of biological development and organization from the formlessness of Universal Intelligence to physical form through the life cycle of growth and changes back into the formlessness of Transformation in the context of Cura Healing Convergence.

Figure 2.1
Body: Formlessness into Form

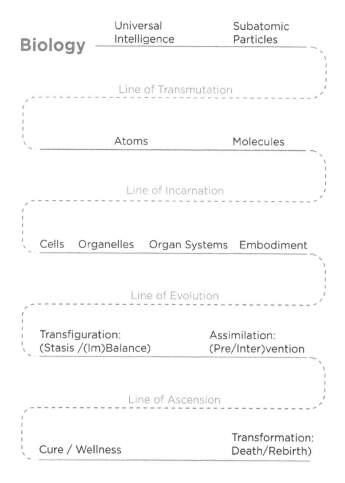

© Dr. Jill Strom, Cura Integrative

So the body and its biological principles begin with the understanding that You = Matter.

Your biological body is created and controlled by both energy and matter. This means your physical existence is rooted in the formless world of Quantum Physics. It means that at the beginning of your formation, there was a point in time when Lifeforce energy emanated through the tissues with consciousness at the **Line of Incarnation,** and your Life was formed. It means that throughout your entire Life, you are matter constantly being created, constantly evolving into a mixture of new and mature cellular matter. It means your existence is also part of the whole picture of dimensional creation. Your body is created and controlled by both energy and matter. The Divine Intelligence of natural order emanates through energy with the unique consciousness of You.

Like the ever-expanding Universe, you, too, are ever-becoming. What is true for the Universe can be applied holographically to everything in it. In 1967, Arthur Koestler, author of *The Ghost in the Machine,* described the human condition as a holarchy: what is true for the whole is true for the part.[11] Koestler's *holon,* an independent, self-reliant part that is also part of a whole, works like a bubble within a bubble. If you've noticed how waterdrops on a leaf show a complete dimensional reflection of the scene around it, you've seen a holon. The facets in a diamond reflect the same way.

Physicist Stephen Hawking elevated the concept to quantum realms in the 1990s with his theory that the Universe is holographic.[12]

The key is recognizing that whatever happens to any part of our body happens to it as a whole, and vice versa. In our bodies, each organelle is whole within itself, and part of a larger cell.

A cell is whole within itself and part of a larger organism. This principle can be extrapolated across atoms to molecules, hearts to minds, even words to sentences. People to groups and groups to societies. Societies to nations; nations to the world. The world to the cosmos: all holons . . . all *both/and* . . . part and whole simultaneously.

This is why Lipton says, "You are, in truth, a cooperative community of approximately fifty trillion single-celled citizens." Each of our cells functions autonomously within the cooperative dynamics of our physiology individually and as a whole.

One part affects the whole; the whole reflects each cell. There will be a time when the health, vitality, and strength of the body is suffering. Stress, disease, pathology—any variable(s) will arise to challenge our homeostasis. We will, at some point, have to act and interact when our internal and external environments stress us. This stress can derive physiologically, energetically, and/or spiritually—all affect the body. All challenge the host. All require the body to assimilate interventions to change, alter, detox, strengthen, and heal.

Without that restoration, too much stress, too much toxicity, too much *dis*-ease, and the body will be challenged to make changes, alter its physiology, and evolve from a state of weakness. We may be unable to balance under such conditions. The body may begin to deteriorate or even deconstruct.

How we respond proactively or reactively in those situations can alter the outcome. How we view our circumstances, and when or if we change our mind about our approach—if we really make a shift—we are, in fact, changing the growth trajectory of every cell in our entire body.

At the cellular level, growth is a continuous process. Energy is constantly forming into matter again and again, generating and regenerating. Cells reproduce themselves instantly. They are in constant creation mode. Additionally, the epigenetic variables provide more opportunity to influence what we are creating in our body and health.

The epigenome, the protein structure surrounding each DNA helix, is altered by our internal and external environment by circumstances including diet, lifestyle, and a host of other influences. As philosopher Eva Jablonka and biologist Marion Lamb wrote in Epigenetic Inheritance and Evolution: The Lamarckian Dimension, "In recent years, molecular biology has shown that the genome is far more fluid and responsive to the environment than previously supposed. It has also shown that information can be transmitted to descendants in ways other than through the base sequence of DNA."[13]

Autonomic creation and *re*creation—this is the natural order, and our greatest asset in the process of regaining homeostasis. If you've ever had the stomach flu, you were no doubt glad that it only takes 24 hours for cells to regenerate the lining of the gut. The liver can regenerate itself within six months.

Cell generation creates organs, and regeneration makes it possible for organs to heal. From subatomic properties to organ systems, each level adds complexity. Between the levels, from cells to tissues, organs to organ systems, we have a series of *layers* of the body. The body is comprised of eleven major organ systems, all operating in part and in whole with the natural order of their design. The largest organ of the human body, the skin, takes a year to fully regenerate. The skin is the body's most important detoxifying organ. It comes in contact with everything in our environment, a most-effective barrier between self and non-self.

Under the skin and throughout the layers of organ systems is a crystalline matrix of connective tissue called fascia. Fascia is a thin sheath of fibrous tissue that surrounds every muscle, muscle fiber, organ, bone, nerve and nerval tissue. This fascia also forms every ligament and tendon within the body as well as all of the internal organs including the heart, lungs, brain, and spinal cord. Fascia is one continuous structure that exists throughout the entire body without interruption.

When our body experiences illness, trauma, scarring, inflammation or emotional insult, we tense up—as if preparing to take the force of the blow whether physical or emotional. If the sickness isn't cured or the threat continues—whether literally or psychically—we may hold that tension in an acute state for hours, days, or even decades. The stress to the fascial system affects the flow of Qi (an Eastern term meaning "flowing energy" or Lifeforce) through the entire body, moving, diverting, and blocking energy. A stressed fascial system loses its elasticity and viscosity, weakening the entire musculoskeletal system, and by extension, all systems.

The musculoskeletal system provides support, stability, and movement to the body. It is comprised of bones, muscles, ligaments, tendons, joints and other connective tissues that support and bind tissues and organs together.

The craniosacral system nourishes the spinal cord and cerebellum. It has its own pulsating rhythm, different from the respiratory rhythm of the body. Balance in the fascial plane lines and cranial sacral rhythm of the body directly helps to stabilize the autonomic nervous system.

Embedded within the physical form is the Central Nervous System that regulates all functions of the body. It includes the Autonomic Nervous System comprised of the Sympathetic (fight, flight, or freeze) and the Parasympathetic (rest, digest, reproduce) functions of the body.

The Nervous Systems regulates the communication of mind-body connection and helps to operate organ system functions. Each of our eleven organ systems has a specific purpose. All operate within the body as a part and as whole. Dysfunction of any one system affects all systems.

Much of Western medicine focuses on the part—the spectrum between cellular function and organ systems. Many doctors will specialize in a specific system: cardiovascular, respiratory, reproductive, etc. They spend hours studying pathology—how that system broke down. Their intervention strategy is procedural or surgical, and/or prescriptive of the right pharmaceutical applications to alter, block, shut down, or tonify specific cellular reactions or organ system functions.

Our medical culture emphasizes specialization, which is a marvelous advancement that makes many things possible, except that it inherently excludes the bigger picture. And there is no true, lasting cure of the part if the whole isn't also healed. An integrated approach isn't superfluous, it is the only scientifically viable approach to true healing . . . to *Cura* at all levels.

Consider how both science and spirit inform our understanding of sickness. The phrase *Let there be Light* speaks to an illuminating brightness that is as literal as it is symbolic. Light energy as electromagnetic waves is brighter when light-waves intensify in vibration or frequency. As the vibration slows, the light dims. Those scientific dynamics apply to energy in its many forms. Just as low-ebbing, slow wave vibrations dim the light until darkness results from the absence of electromagnetic light waves, low energy in the body can be caused by the absence of light, both literally and symbolically.

This is literally, scientifically accurate, as well as metaphorically and transfiguratively true.

Just as darkness results from the absence of light, negative-dark events like sickness, disease, trauma, and insult lower the energy frequency of the body. If the energy of the body continues to remain low or decrease over a period of time, the change in energy transfigures the body into more matter and less energy. It begins to abide by the laws of Newtonian Physics. The body acts more like a particle and less like a wave. It becomes vulnerable and breaks down to disease and aging.

The chakras, our body's energy centers, are whirling and spiraling with Qi energy, moving in a circadian rhythm: chest to hands, hands to head, head to feet, feet to chest. Every two hours, this clock-like cycle flows through our entire fascial system along energetic pathways or meridians.

Qi energy flows through the conduit of our body's meridians. When that circulation is compromised by denser matter and less energy, the Qi slows down, diverts, or moves restrictively. Those meridians can be compromised by illness, injury, or insult including things we might not have considered: plastic surgery, implantations, laser hair removal, or even humiliation, shock, and grief. Any alteration in homeostasis can block the channels for self-healing and self-regulating systems of the body. Modifying or altering the energy meridians of the body creates a scarring denseness—whether physical or emotional—that is more correlated and connected to denser matter.

Kinesiology exposed, for the first time, the intimate connection between the mind and the body, revealing that the mind 'thinks' with the body itself. Therefore, it provided an avenue for the exploration of the ways consciousness reveals itself in the subtle mechanisms behind the disease process.
– David R. Hawkins, MD, PhD[14]

Bioenergetics, the science of energy transformation in living things, describes the chemistry of that process. In terms of medicine and healing, we cannot think of the body in pathological terms strictly as dense physical matter. In doing so, we miss the multidimensionality. We miss the miraculous potential of energy. We miss the creative, regenerative healing that is available to us. We miss the fullness of who we are as an individual, only experiencing and addressing the holon as part, not the holographic reality.

There is a healthy way to be ill.
- George Sheehan

Illness isn't always a bad thing, just as darkness isn't always negative. Darkness promotes the circadian rhythms of sleep and restoration for all living things. It is the business day of nocturnal lifeforms. Darkness provides the balance, and even the ability to recognize light because of the dimensions in shadow that it creates. So, too, does *dis*-ease serve a purpose.

The natural design of Universal Intelligence clearly encompasses a function for disease. Disease creates certain possibilities as our immune system can be strengthened by the diseases and sickness it overcomes. In this autonomic process, we have a proactive role to play.

There is a moment when a person can choose a higher vibration or a lower vibration. Energy or particle. Quanta or dust. The virtues of positive thinking aside, the physiological impact literally produces a hormonal, chemical reaction that fuels our Qi.

When we focus on positive thoughts, intentions, and prayers, there are neuropeptides that activate a hormonal center prompting the neurochemistry of our body to release a cascade of "feel good" hormones like dopamine and serotonin. Our alpha and theta brain wave activity shows an altered state of consciousness. We are bio-energetically conducive to respond accordingly: to rest, digest, or reproduce.

From stasis to change, our epigenetics are constantly transfiguring the physical, dimensional aspects of our biology. Traditionally, certain undesirable changes are anticipated with preventative measures or met with medical interventions— both in hopes of maintaining or achieving wellness. Our form is transfigured in that process, and what we *were* is literally new—new cells, new skin, new strength.

Our visage, too, is also altered by new perspectives on what it means to be human. The maiden will pass when the mother becomes . . . that the boy will end when a man is ready to be. Every new thing is a beginning, and all beginnings mark the end of what was. **Transfiguration** (see Figure 2.1) is, by design, the process wherein we become unrecognizable to what we once were. We no longer relate, except historically, to what was once our own identity.

To assimilate the biological imperative to change is a normal process. Even when it involves negative-dark feelings and outcomes, it is growth and evolution. Changes in our bodies are by Divine design. They are part of a process of evolution stemming from normal development, or a crisis of growth—including disease. Regardless of what interventions and influences are engaged through these changes, true transformation happens after we have ascended beyond the literal circumstances to grasp the wisdom that makes us stronger because of the experience. Whether our biological life as we know it continues or not, crossing the **Line of Ascension** will compel **Transformation** with death and rebirth—something ends and something else begins. (See Figure 2.1)

There are symbolic endings and literal ones. When literal death of the body happens, we struggle to accept it. In our culture, both medically and culturally, physical death is rarely treated as an acceptable outcome when it results from sickness. Somewhere in society we normalized end-of-life care to mean lengthen-life care, sometimes regardless of the quality of that life. At all times, it was the job of medicine to keep the body going.

There are times when the Cura involves a life healed, saved. And there are times when the cycle of life has come to an end. Naturally. Holistically. Death may also be true healing if the energy of that life is ready for Transformation.

From a holistic point of view, we are ever-becoming, ever-creating, and there is a natural cycle from birth to death to rebirth. So death is understood to be a vital part of the multidimensionality of our life cycle; not just biologically, but spiritually and energetically as well.

Sometimes into death, sometimes into new life; Death is always a process that cycles one form of energy to another. However it happens, it is both spiritually and scientifically true that the energy of the body goes back into formlessness. The Divine Intelligence that informs life will re-create form from formless energy.

Death is not the end—it is **Transformation**. It is **Conversion** and **Re-Creation**. It is an individual consciousness ascending to full and Unitive Consciousness. (See Figure 2.1) There is no end, literally. There is no end spiritually or scientifically. Whatever part of us is ashes and dust is also a holon and whole in the Universal Lifeforce. The essence of something, the energy of it, is never lost. It only changes form. Therefore, death is a transformation of form . . . the next beginning that always follows the end.

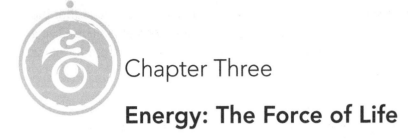

Chapter Three

Energy: The Force of Life

There is a place where all things begin.
A moment when time starts.
A space where the formless comes into form.
Creation. The Word. Evolution. The Big Bang.

Let there be Light.

A beginning.

There have been many theories around this very conceptus. Regardless of the semantics of creation, in its rawest inalienable form, in the beginning was pure energy: the **Universal Lifeforce**. Where that energy came from and why or how it evolved into physical form has been theorized by many diverse schools of thought from Biblical authors to Lamarck to Einstein.

One constant remains true: energy is in all things. All things begin somehow and some place for a reason—whether scientific or spiritual or both—and all things have an ending.

Energy.

Energy's function is more expansive than our common assumptions about it. Energy is at work in ways we are only just beginning to grasp. From the power created by sun, wind, or water, to the combustion of fossil fuel, to the electrical signatures emitted by flowers to attract bumblebees, energy is at work. Even the chemistry felt between two people is the conduction of energy.

The spectrum of energy is infinite. So the terms in which we speak about it, the laws by which we measure it, and the understanding we have of it need to also adhere to an infinite spectrum.

Science has taken us part of the way there.

In the early 1900s, the discovery of electromagnetic phenomena led to the concept of Field Theory that delineated the two energy dynamics of physics: Classical and Quantum. Classical Field Theory predicts how one or more physical fields interact with matter through field equations, most commonly: polarity, velocity, or gravity. Quantum Field Theory predicts how the energy of matter has the potential and tendency to manifest as physical reality. The subjectivity of that is key. Quantum Field Theory presents staggering implications for diagnostics and treatment, possibilities just now being explored by Western medicine. Given the potential and tendency for sickness and disease to manifest as physical reality, it is imperative to look into the quantum nature of their origins—at the level of energy.

Acknowledging the depth and breadth of quantum realities calls into question the philosophical foundations of traditional medical practice and health care systems. This change in perspective would require an approach that recognizes the universe and everything in it as forms of energy that create, act upon, affect and are affected by other energy forms.

What would it look like if we delved into the spectrum of energy to provide an explanation for sickness and disease?

All forms of energy are, by definition, either *kinetic* or *potential.*

Kinetic is energy that comes from movement—like a waterfall cascading or a hammer hitting a nail; it is in a person dancing and in a heart beating. It is energy happening.

Potential energy is that contained in the position or condition of a static body—like a rock perched perilously on a ledge, or even holding back words that need to be spoken.

Kinetic energy is movement, and potential energy is energy in the possibility of movement.

It is both the work that's being done and the capacity to do work. It is a *both/and* reality

Physical Science teaches us that all living things are made up of matter and that there are levels of organization that make up the world as we know it. Protons, neutrons, and electrons join to make atoms, which form into cells; cells form into organs, organs into organ systems, and so on and so forth. All have their own properties and dynamics in **Newtonian Science**. These levels of organization are presented as basic biological truth.

Which they are—but only the basics. The ambiguous potential of **Quantum Physics** is rarely taught with the same merit and assurance as Newtonian Physics. Yet quanta (the plural of quantum) is the essence of the universe . . . *the vast energy before manifestation of matter.*

Quanta has no mass and no electrical charge. It is the smallest unit of energy (that we know of) that exists within and between the particles that make up the atoms that make up the cells that eventually form our organ systems. It is infinitesimal, but measurable and extremely important.

In 1900, Max Planck, the father of modern Physics, developed the Planck constant that delineated light as both a wavelength (formlessness) and as a particle (form) in its smallest, indivisible units known as *quanta*. That discovery meant quanta could be measured. In 1905, Einstein explained the relationship between energy and matter: when energy (as wavelength) is slowed down enough to form a particle (matter), it is expressed as $E = MC^2$.[15]

Simply stated, energy and matter are interconvertible.

Consider how this applies to light energy. Light is both a wavelength (energy) and a particle (matter). Under conditions of interference and refraction, light demonstrates properties of a wavelength. Yet under conditions of emission or absorption, light exhibits the properties of a particle, emitting one photon at a time. In essence, light is simultaneously *both/and*, not *either/or* energy/matter.

"Either/or" Newtonian perceptions of our reality—what can be proven as true or not true that characterizes this historical approach to knowledge—are both myopic and, sometimes, inaccurate. We live in a Quantum *both/and* universe. The Universe is energy and matter—we are both energy and matter. These are simultaneous realities. They are complementary, if paradoxical. This greater understanding of universal dynamics is vitally important to our knowledge and applications in medicine and healing. It marks the **Line of Transmutation** where energy converts to matter when prompted by the force of creation (more about that in Chapter Five).

Biologically speaking, life begins when matter is organized into a form. Laws that direct the embodiment of energy were first articulated by theoretical physicist Albert Einstein.

Einstein proved there is a point of manifestation when energy slows down enough to become a particle in this dimensional existence; when a wavelength elongates, slowing down enough to become matter. There is also a discrete unit (amount) of energy that most physicists call rest mass energy. It is the most fundamental, quantifiable amount of energy that is needed to create a particle . . . to create matter. So with the right vibration of a quantifiable amount, energy converts to matter.

In the Cura context, this conversion happens at the **Line of Transmutation**. This line delineates the formless into form. Once transmuted, our quantum energy then exists in mass—a tangible quantity of **Universal Lifeforce** embodied and measurable in Physical Science. The particle that creates the tangible body that is you, is ever becoming from a state of energy. You are an energetic wavelength slowing itself down to continuously manifest as a particle, and yet, constantly vibrating as a wavelength. You are both the energy and the embodiment of energy. Not only that, energy is constantly forming into matter again and again and forever again. Therefore, you are constantly being created anew.

Everything is energetic before it manifests physically, or biologically. Each of us is an embodiment of energy with our own singular vibration. We are comprised of atoms—of matter that was created under the conditions that transmuted formlessness into form. "Quantum physicists discovered that physical atoms are made up of vortices of energy that are constantly spinning and vibrating; each atom is like a wobbly spinning top that radiates energy. Because each atom has its own specific energy signature (wobble), assemblies of atoms (molecules) collectively radiate their own identifying energy patterns. So every material structure in the universe, including you and me, radiates a unique energy signature," writes quantum physicist Bruce Lipton.[16]

The energy signature of our physical form includes the unique, individual consciousness that is you. You are embodying energy in constant motion formed into matter. You are an expression that exists uniquely in the realm of physical science as *you*, but also as an expression and extension of the Universal Lifeforce. Dense Matter. And yet, you still vibrate.

You are still a wavelength of light energy in motion.

You are still quanta.

You are still coming into being.

You are becoming.

Part of that energy you are embodying, the energy that is you—the Lifeforce of your being—is known as *Qi*.

In Eastern medicine, **Qi** (pronounced "chi") is the energy in and around our bodies including tangible, tactile forms that do the work of being conscious and alive. Every heartbeat is a tangible form of energy conductance.

According to research done at the HeartMath Institute, "We know the heartbeat begins with a pulse of electricity through the heart muscle. This electricity arises because of a large number of charged particles flow across the muscle membranes to excite contraction. These currents also spread out into surrounding tissues. Some of the flow of electricity is through the circulatory system, which is an excellent conductor of electricity because of its high salt content. As the circulation carries blood to every tissue, heart electricity flows everywhere in the body. Hence the electrocardiogram can be picked up anywhere on the skin, even from the toes."[17]

Figure 3.1 shows how our Energy as Lifeforce creates and flows through the physical form as Qi. Once science understood energy at the level of Quantum Physics, a lexicon for describing the process by which Universal Lifeforce becomes an individual life form developed, although Eastern medicine has long understood this dynamic.

Figure 3.1
Energy: The Incarnation of Universal Lifeforce

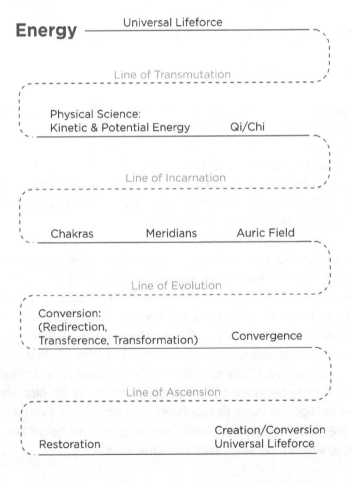

The very present but intangible ways in which our Qi manifests affect points of our body uniquely. Throughout our bodies, unique *chakras* are localizing specific tasks. **Chakras** are subtle energy centers that emit radiant energy.

Qi energy circulates through our bodies, moving through each chakra along pathways akin to the central nervous system known as *meridians*. **Meridians** are energetic pathways through the matrix of fascia, the membrane that holds the physical form together.

Just as the nervous systems looks essentially the same in every body, the meridians also present uniformly in the body. Traditional Chinese medicine has studied these meridians and utilized them in acupuncture for over a thousand years.

The normal, healthy flow of Qi sustains life in the collective, organized matter that makes up our body. The unobstructed surge of Qi, or the degree to which it is blocked, determines the health and vitality of an individual.

The interruption of our Lifeforce energy can be caused by many things; healing always involves the restoration of healthy Qi flow. When Qi is diverted or blocked, disease states can arise.

Various degrees of blockage equate to various disease states. Superficial cuts, scars, and piercings can all affect or even block the energy flow through meridians. In some cases, energy will divert around a piercing or an abrasion, but deeper wounds may create a significant blockage.

Emotional trauma, aberrant thoughts, or depression will also disrupt the energy flow and directly affect the function of the individual. Environments (physical or mental), relationships, stress, and exposure to negative energy can also deplete energy within and around a person, and even create blockages that leave energetic wounds or scars.

If Qi is in dangerously low supply—as may be the case in comatose or in certain disembodied situations—we may not be "clinically dead," but our bodies cannot animate. When Lifeforce has "passed on," the energy that was that person has converted but it has not ended. Again, the laws of science state that energy doesn't "die," it only changes form.

Our energy is not wholly contained within our body. Qi energy emanates around our physical form creating an **Auric Field,** as it is known in Eastern traditions. Have you ever noticed how you felt better around an upbeat, pleasant person but anxious or sad around a depressive personality? We are profoundly affected by another's energy level— for better or for worse. "The heart's electromagnetic field is by far the most powerful produced by the body; it is approximately five thousand times greater in strength than the field produced by the brain. Furthermore, research from The HeartMath Research Institute indicates that energetic information entrained in the heart's field isn't detected only by our own brains and bodies but can also be registered by the people around us."[18]

This speaks to the subjectivity of quantum realities: the influence of our own energy, our thoughts, feelings, and emotions, and the energy of all light and matter relative to the situation including the people, place, and things around us, can and do alter the dynamics of a given physical reality. They are the variables that prompt conversion of energy into matter—this is the stuff of creation and re-creation. What we consciously create (or unconsciously allow to be created) prompts the embodiment that happens at the Line of Transmutation.

The multidimensional implications of this are vast in terms of healing. We must recognize that our energy is ever-creating, always-embodying our physical form. The forces at work in this process—both scientific and spiritual—are manifesting the reality we create. In integrative medicine, a practitioner's inquiry should take a look into all dimensional realities of the patient, which will be addressed in *Chapter Eight: Cura Consciousness.*

Much of the medical field—and much of society—disregard energetic explanations or energy-healing modalities because there is no substantial research to prove their effectiveness. But what is not regularly questioned or considered is that traditional methods are not focused on and possibly not capable of research into aspects beyond the scope of Newtonian Physics. Further, by its very nature, Quantum Physics shows how difficult it is to accurately predict or replicate outcomes given the variable of energy. In 1927, Werner Heisenberg proved that research itself is influenced by the act of being observed. Known as the *Heisenberg Effect*, this is the phenomenon of human presence altering the energy and movement of particles, which subsequently alters the outcome of the experiment.[19]

As new and profound advances in science have deepened and broadened our understanding of both human physiology and Quantum Physics, the integration of this information challenges and changes our perspectives of life, health, and the universe.

Science is now utilizing more advanced technology and proving theories that were acknowledged by Einstein, Planck, and even Plato. What we create at the level of energy manifests at the level of biology. This is not new science, this is convergence—science and energy . . . Cataphatic and Apophatic perspectives working together.

**I used the word "God" like Einstein did,
as a shorthand for the laws of physics.
– Stephen Hawking**

Health professions have been greatly challenged to accept the dimensional implications that emerging science is proving. This multidimensional reality calls into question our medical paradigm—not only of human physiology, but also the evolutionary power of our mind, our creative processes, and our divine spirit, which we'll explore in Chapter Four.

Life is more than matter. Our bodies are more than matter. The physical form, animate or inanimate, is more than matter. As the embodiment of energy, the restoration of health involves going back to the start—back to the energy of **creation**, **conversion**, and **regeneration**.

Energy is never lost,[20] it only alters its form in three ways:

- Redirection (from its original trajectory)
- Transfer (from one thing to another)
- Transform (from one form into another)

Ever since that apple fell on Isaac Newton's head, its apple-energy has continued to redirect, transfer, and transform things on earth in ways the father of Newtonian Science could never have imagined. It gave him food as fuel, a bump on the head, and a transformative idea. To grasp what forces are at play in this never-ending dynamic of creation, we must approach it with *both/and* thinking.

Energy works both subjectively and objectively on the mind and body.

When we make the connection that energy is influencing our condition, and that we can choose the energy we allow into that process, we are making conscious choices that can alter, redirect, and/or transmute the outcome. We become consciously engaged in the creation process that transmutes energy into matter.

This can come from internal shifts of thought, releasing stored emotions, changing the nutrients we feed our physical form, or altering the environment in which we find ourselves. It is no small thing to change the course of disease by identifying and influencing the energy that feeds it. It may require spending more time outdoors or changing the music that we listen to; or it could mean quitting a job or leaving an abusive relationship. What's happening when we make intentional changes is a very big thing—it's Quantum big.

Consider this: people get better. They heal even from the direst diseases without drugs or surgery. When medicine or science cannot explain why, an explanation often provided is the "placebo effect." By definition, placebo is a substance having no pharmacological effect, although patients given a placebo may show improvement in their medical condition. Quantum Physics provides a greater understanding of what is really happening in this dynamic process.

The placebo works because a person accepts and believes in a known remedy—a fake pill, injection, or procedure substituted for its real counterpart—and then surrenders to the outcome without over-analyzing how it's going to happen. We could say that a person associates her future experience of a particular known person or thing at a specific time and place in her external

> **environment with a change in her internal
> environment, and in doing so, she alters her
> state of being.** – Joe Dispenza[21]

Altering our state of being is to alter the energy vibration we are emitting and attracting as conduits of the energy we produce. The apple, the music, the hug, and our thoughts are all emitting energy. The quality of that energy is affected by the environment and the conduit through which it travels, i.e., our bodies. Our bodies are a conduit, both mechanically (as a physical medium) and radiantly (electromagnetically) receiving and expressing energy.

What does all this have to do with placebos, healing, and Isaac Newton? In short, everything. The convergence of Eastern and Western medicine—of Newtonian Science and Quantum Physics—solves for the fact that **energy itself is the missing link,** the X factor.

> **Everything is energy and that's all
> there is to it. Match the frequency of the
> reality you want and you cannot help but
> get that reality. It can be no other way.
> This is not philosophy. This is physics.**
> – Albert Einstein

The quality of energy has everything to do with our life and our wellness. We have the ability to affect the quality of our energy, and we must take responsibility for our role in that process. True healing requires engagement at every level—including especially the level of energy.

Energy is both quantitative and qualitative. The quantity and quality of energy is affected objectively and subjectively, internally and externally. It is a multi-dimensional proceeding.

It is ever-unfolding and creating. Understanding how this works relative to our health requires us to think of ourselves—our bodies and minds—as part of the scientific equation. We take mechanical and radiant energy in to live, which means we are transforming, redirecting, and transferring it as a matter of scientific fact. As the conduit, we are very much part of the equation.

Radiant and mechanical energy can transfer, redirect, and transmute in the elements of air, water, earth, and fire. Because humans, plants, and animals are made of material and elemental properties, we are all conduits for energy. Energy travels through us as readily as electric current flows through wire, and radiant sun energy feeds growing plants. We carry our own energy and exchange energy with others including plants and animals. We absorb and are altered by the influence of the energy around us. The quality of our energy—the frequency at which we vibrate with high or low energy—attracts like energy back to us. We are permeable to the influence of some, but not all, energy based on that law of attraction and repulsion.

Many factors influence permeability including (but not limited to):

- Diet and Lifestyle
- Work and Relationships
- Family and Community
- Health, Stress and Rest
- Genetics and Epigenetics

Our receptivity to the energy around us varies greatly. If we are willing and aware, the energy of persons or the synergy of a situation can greatly influence our physical and mental state according to how conducive (or conductive) we are. We are literally conducting the flow of that energy, which can alter the way our Qi is moving (or not moving) productively through our body.

Likewise, we can **redirect, transfer, or transform** energy within us based on our thoughts, feelings, and emotions. We can change, create and transform our own energy, and thus our own body, health, and vitality.

This is the power we possess individually and collectively on the vast, multidimensional continuum of creation. It is the fusion of our Lifeforce with the Universal Intelligence contained in each cell of our mind-body connection. It is the energetic and biologic merging in the great mystery of creation. It is the multidimensional process that works synergistically in healing.

This is where all things begin and where all things return in the cycle of energy. From its genesis to its exodus, through conversion and regeneration of Lifeforce, energy itself makes the embodiment of Spirit *(Universal Intelligence)* possible.

Chapter 4

Evolution: A Spiritual Imperative

Everything is spiritual.
- Rob Bell

In truth, everything is spiritual.

Which means everything pertains, is relative to, and affects the soul, our immortal essence.

Everything.

Our essence and our being is spiritual, which is to say we matter and our lives have meaning beyond literal existence . . . beyond our own understanding. According to natural laws ordered by something greater than ourselves that we have named Divine, our lives have purpose. We are energetically, physiologically, and purposefully expressed by **Divine Intelligence** in a universe in and from which all individual souls are created and shall return. Ashes to ashes . . . dust to stardust.

Spirit speaks in many different ways, one of which is the body. The body is the place of our spirit's residence—our temple. It grounds us to the physical world while serving as a means of communication with the Divine. It allows us to physically feel the agony and ecstasy, the weight of the world as well as our own response across the range of emotions. The body is a mechanism for spiritual awakening.

Incarnation prompts us to search for meaning and purpose. We are physical beings infused with a Divine spirit that is always at work bringing our literal existence into harmony with the purpose and calling of our life.

> **The goal of life is to make our heartbeat match the beat of the universe. To match your nature with Nature. – Joseph Campbell**

Our thoughts, feelings, and emotions arising uniquely from our personal experience and understood in context to our spiritual self-awareness constitute our consciousness.

Your individual consciousness is connected to the **Collective Unconscious** of all existence. In Jungian terms, the Collective Unconscious is the innate, intuitive, and instinctive understanding of common truths universally shared by all sentient beings. It is expressed in archetype, mythology, dreams, and symbolism.

In every language and culture, there is an inclination to personify and name the Divine: Great Spirit. God. Goddess. Mother-Father God. Heavenly Father. Elohim. Ilah. Elah. Allah, Yahweh. Also, there is recognition that this force cannot be named: YHWH. All Knowing. The Word. Higher Power. All Powerful. Almighty. Creator. Universe. In Jungian terms, **Universal Consciousness**—all that is known, that can be known, and everything beyond our comprehension—also applies.

Out of this great, vast void of creative potential that is Universal Consciousness, the "personal consciousness" (as Carl Jung termed it) emerges in each and every individual at the **Line of**

Incarnation when energy manifests in a unique physical form. The Spirit made into the flesh of *You.*

You, me, all of us are "made in the image of God." The Divine. The great I AM energy of an Individual (Ego) embodied (em*Body*'ed) with Spirit because *the Word was God made flesh* (in the Christian tradition, per John 1, NIV).

Our life's work—the fulfillment of our purpose on earth—involves coming into greater consciousness as a wholly divine individual. Each of us is called to that work . . . the course is always set towards wholeness. Each misstep is an opportunity to explore the distance between ourselves and the Divine, and to make a better choice with greater self-awareness next time. With each intentional step, we are waking up (becoming conscious) to remember who we truly are, and to comprehend the spiritual power we possess in creating our reality.

> **As spiritual adults, we accept responsibility for co-creating our lives and our health. Co-creation is in fact the essence of spiritual adulthood: it is the exercise of choice and the acceptance of our responsibility for those choices. – Caroline Myss**

Consciousness is the dynamic state of intelligence, intention, awareness, and self-awareness.

With that awareness, we think and act. Thoughts are creative. Words are creative. We are creative.

Therein lies the power.

> **With every action, comment, and conversation, we have the choice to invite Heaven or Hell to Earth. – Rob Bell**

Your thinking and doing—what you choose to focus on and the meaning you give to it—literally energizes waves of probability into particles of manifestation. Into this life and this world that you know and experience, you create a reality that informs (for better or worse) the **Collective Unconscious** and the Universal Consciousness of Being. It is the Universal Lifeforce driving the co-creative process that joins Divine Intelligence to the potential of each of us as Word-Made-Flesh to express our best and highest thinking and doing.

Being.

By design, this is a perfectly imperfect process.

We all create our own reality. From *sensa* (sensory-input), we attach meaning that creates what we come to believe or know about what we have experienced. From that perspective, we perceive reality—it becomes real, tangible, *sensate*. Our consciousness informs our purpose. Sometimes, maybe even much of the time, we get it wrong because we are still learning. Much of the time, we learn what we are by discovering what we are not. That is a process of trial and error.

Sometimes a life's purpose is to change the course of history. Sometimes that purpose is to raise conscious children. Sometimes that purpose is to support another in need, or to allow ourselves to be supported. Whatever are our *Sacred Contracts,*[22] there are lessons to be learned, experiences to be had, karma to be balanced, and some calling to be fulfilled that is unique to each of us. Every aspect of this, every moment of heart beating, there is a Divine imperative to evolve spiritually.

The inspiration to evolve spiritually is already a manifestation of the presence of God within, and it's certainly indicative of

good karma. Just to want to know truth, to evolve, to improve oneself, to become a better person, to fulfill one's potential—those are all inspirations. And the person doesn't make them up; they just come to them. It's like an innate desire to fulfill your potential. That potential as one evolves becomes more and more identified in spirituality—the capacity to love, to forgive, to appreciate, to see the beauty in all that exists, to live in peace and harmony instead of discord and strife [...] The only requirement is to do whatever you do to the best of your capacity and leave the rest up to God. – David R. Hawkins, MD, PhD [23]

Throughout life, situations or circumstances arise that compel greater mindfulness and spiritual consciousness. Everyone we meet is a teacher along the way. Every life circumstance is an avenue for learning. We are called to the cutting edge of growth where we must evolve. We must change or accept (consciously or unconsciously) the consequences of resistance, stagnation, acceptance, or surrender. Sometimes this is prompted by some kind of crisis. Sickness and disease are common events that propel us to move across the **Line of Evolution**.

We evolve, individually, and/or collectively, depending on the choice that was made to grow (or not). All change affects us individually, and those around us holographically.

This can be a change in a cultural norm (think: Gandhi) or a change in personal perspective. Ideally, we get the message, we learn the lesson. We change our job, our relationship(s), our diet, our church, or our attitude. It can look like a complete overhaul of life, or a profoundly different internal landscape.

Changing the way we choose to view our circumstances can recalibrate our vibrational frequency and our reality. And we grow in enlightenment. **Enlightenment** is not a destination, it is a continuum—a consequence, an intention, and a lifestyle.

As David R. Hawkins, MD, PhD, wrote, "The seeking of Enlightenment is a very major commitment, and is, in fact, the most difficult of human pursuits. It can be alternately arduous or exhilarating, exciting or tedious, demanding or inspiring. There are great breakthroughs as well as exasperating, seemingly impossible obstacles. It is to be expected that this pattern is par for the course."[24]

Few of us go willingly into change. We tend to avoid the lesson rather than do the hard work of higher consciousness. We move on too fast. Or we refuse to move at all and stagnate in our comfort zone. It's easier to deal with the devil we know than the devil we don't know. So we fixate; we attach to the past or to fear, or we unconsciously miss the mark. We "descend" into darkness: addiction, depression, or the next distraction or detour off the path of our growth.

> **When we resist change, it's called suffering.
> But when we can completely let go and not
> struggle against it, when we can embrace
> the groundlessness of our situation and
> relax into its dynamic quality, that's called
> enlightenment. – Pema Chödrön**

Opting out of growth is often an unconscious process. We may be unaware of the fact that the reality we are living was not consciously chosen, but simply adopted or adapted from the tribe. "Reality" is uninformed by the truth of a personal, individual consciousness. We don't think our own thoughts;

we remain part of group-think, which is by its very nature survivalist and fear-based.

In those situations, we react the way we have always reacted. Therefore, the outcome never changes. Unconsciously, we recreate the same circumstances at their equivalent vibration which grows heavier with each repeated, unresolved event. Again and again, the dynamics of our lives unfold to teach the same lesson in a larger, more difficult way, as though evolution itself was pressing more urgently for growth, which indeed it is.

Other times, we have that *aha* moment. We see clearly, or more clearly. We gain insight, or a greater perspective. We release the past: the hurt, resentment, or energetic-burden we've been carrying. We may experience the same circumstances but respond differently, more consciously than we did before. We experience them yet again, but only in the distant story of another. Until behind us, we see the rings of the labyrinth through which we've been moving. We recognize slow but steady progress, not just the circling of the lost. We gain a greater personal truth and we come into greater wholeness with ourselves and/or with God. We are contributing higher vibrations to the reservoir of the Collective Unconscious; we ascend in our vibration to levels of transformation and healing.

Jane's Story

I grew up in a loving family, the fourth of four daughters, followed by my brother, the baby of the family. My parents had very strong values for church and family. Their high expectations and intense nurturing produced five successful, dutiful adults who always did what was asked of them with a smile on their face. Our family was admired by many church people and family friends, but the programming of my youth left me with some important themes that were unaddressed. If you must always be happy, what do you do with your unhappiness? If you have to do what everyone asks of you, how do you know how to say no?

It was difficult for me to reconcile an understanding of how my "happy" childhood could result in chronic health issues. It would take years for me to make that connection. And I've come to realize that pain can be an invitation to healing on many levels; it is an inextricable part of a process called birth whether literal or symbolic.

I gave birth to three amazing, talented, hilarious, handsome, creative, intelligent sons—a process as excruciatingly painful as it was joyously rewarding. During my pregnancies, I developed plantar fasciitis that was so painful it hindered my mobility. Usually the pain would subside after my babies were born. However, that was not the case after my third pregnancy. My heels were in a great deal of pain, my kneecaps stopped tracking, causing additional joint pain, and then I developed a pelvic tilt. I side-stepped down stairs and walked with much difficulty even as my young boys ran circles around me. I sought traditional medical intervention—physical therapy, orthotics in my shoes, and bi-lateral release knee surgery. Nothing helped.

My husband Rick watched as I struggled with increasingly complex issues: immobility, then severe digestive issues, painful menstruation cycles, fibroids in my uterus, and chronic joint pain. It felt like my body was shutting down on me. On several occasions, he took me to the emergency room when I was in serious distress. He stood by me with love and kindness. He shared my frustration with the lack of answers that we were finding in Western medicine. Without Rick's support, I don't know how I would have had the strength to keep hoping and striving for a better outcome.

As I searched for alternative ways to heal, I discovered a book called Anatomy of the Spirit by Caroline Myss. I read it feverishly for several months trying to understand what was happening in my body as it related to my spirit. I also traveled to several parts of the country to hear Dr. Myss speak. Her message gave me tremendous insight and was key in helping me understand the relationship between mind and body in health.

Over the next few years of study, exploration, and pain management, I shifted between medical interventions and alternative modalities including holistic kinesiology, acupressure, shamanic healing, crystals, and a host of other energy modalities. I was exhausted from trying to find cures for my ailments and exhausted from trying to tell my story to every new practitioner. I often felt alone and misunderstood. No one else that I knew seemed to need this "special" care that I was pursuing. Worse still, I wasn't getting any better.

Not wanting to leave any stone unturned, I went to a clinic offering integrative medicine to learn more about new methods. I met a woman there who read auric fields. She did a brief assessment of my body just by looking at me. Then she described where she saw places that were in pain and where there would be more discomfort if we didn't correct the issues that were already present. She was accurate about every pain, and I was so relieved that someone seemed to genuinely see me and finally understand. She told me about a Chi Master who had moved to the states from China who could help me.

I drove an hour and a half for my first treatment with Master Chen. Not having any idea what to expect, I was nervous and intimidated, and he knew it. Although no words were spoken about my anxiety, he set a chair right by the door so I would feel the freedom to leave at any time if needed. Then he began working on pressure points on my head explaining that treatment isn't always directly needed on the place that hurts. The energies in our body are all connected, and the origin of the problem might not be where the sickness or pain shows up.

As he worked on my head, I felt a sensation in my uterus—as if it were being vacuumed out. My first session with him brought immediate pain relief, and I enthusiastically committed to working with him. Master Chen quickly became my healer, my teacher, and my friend.

What I learned from Master Chen was that the energy in my first three chakras was so blocked that it was causing the lower half of my body to atrophy. Each chakra fuels different parts of the body. For me, the blockage was starving the flow of energy to my lower extremities—like water not reaching the root of a plant. Applying what I knew from Myss's work, I saw my childhood and young womanhood as a fairly unconscious existence. I appeared confident on the outside, and I was, but inside were forces unseen and feelings unfelt. Unconsciously, I was holding the emotional wounds of unexpressed hurt, anger, resentment, and sadness. Although I appeared confident on the inside, I felt unheard, dismissed, and unseen. I raised my head in pride never letting anyone see my pain—including myself. I was literally unconscious to the painful experiences that presented themselves in my life.

My parents believed that coming downstairs in the morning without a smile on your face was unacceptable, so I trained myself to act happy, even when I wasn't. I laughed a lot— even if I felt like crying. Although I believe there is great value in laughter and a positive outlook on life, pretending you're happy when you're not requires an ability to tune out your own feelings. Any time I had an unpleasant feeling, I unconsciously dismissed it or soothed myself with comfort foods to swallow it down. Those were my coping mechanisms. The energy of unacknowledged pain lodged in my uterus and abdominal area causing digestive and menstruation issues, and eventually created structural issues with my legs and feet. My lower chakras became more and more blocked as I happily and unconsciously marched through life making decisions that were not in alignment with my own sense of self . . . with my spirit. Eventually, my body literally stopped me in my tracks. If I couldn't be healed, I would spend the rest of my life in pain in a wheelchair.

Healing came from inside. Master Chen taught me to "go to nothing" in daily meditation. Sitting in silence with myself daily allowed me to begin feeling who I really was inside my "home energy." I would meditate before and after I spent time with other people so that I could see the difference in how I was feeling before and what feelings I experienced after. It took time for me to recognize my own feelings. I became aware that my intuitive nature made me vulnerable to other people's energy—not always in a good way. Professionally, I was a social worker and personally I was the confidante of many friends and family. They felt relieved of their burdens and much better after we had talked, but I often felt worse. I had to learn more about energy management. I had to learn how to offload or deflect the energies that I was absorbing from others. I had to learn a new consciousness— and greater self-awareness. I was discovering what I felt and what I wanted—it was key to my health. My digestive issues improved with an altered diet, and my uterine fibroids dissolved over time. An ultrasound showed no evidence of them after many months of acupuncture. I felt myself coming back to a full life.

At one point after I'd been improving steadily from treatment with Master Chen, I awakened one morning to an excruciating back pain. I had just been to see Chen, so I didn't think that I needed to return to him so quickly. Somehow, I had the awareness to go see the specialist that made the orthotics that I wore in my shoes on a daily basis. He asked me to walk down the hallway of his office in my bare feet. He looked astonished as I walked up and down the hallway. Back down in his office, he sat on the floor in front of me and asked me sincerely what I was doing to heal. I sheepishly pulled my copy of *Anatomy of the Spirit* out of my purse and explained that I was seeing an acupuncturist who was a Chi Master. He just looked at me marveling and said, "Well, you keep doing whatever you're doing because you no longer have a pelvic tilt. Your back is aching because you have orthotics that were made for a person who has one." We laughed excitedly about this change and he made me one last pair of orthotics without the height adjustments. I told him this would be the last pair of orthotics I would need from him, which proved true. I no longer wear orthotics and I never saw him again, but I was so grateful for his openness and encouragement and for keeping me walking when I did need them. I even wrote him a thank you note telling him so!

Master Chen was ultimately responsible for helping me heal, but it was up to me to listen more closely to the Divine Intelligence of my spirit and to change the way I moved through my life in accordance with the direction that I received. Master Chen taught me the necessity of taking care of my own spirit through the choices that I make in my daily life. I learned the importance of a daily meditation practice to stay grounded in myself. Throughout those years of my healing journey, my oldest sister Joan was one of my closest confidantes. Even though we lived in two different cities, we would spend hours on the phone talking through the details of my personal process and about what I was learning about my own spirit. Joan was open and receptive, and I was grateful for her input and support. Coming from a very religious home, we had been taught that we were responsible for the care of others, but we had little practice caring for ourselves. Turning the focus inward seemed selfish at best. It took me a long time to learn that self-love was a necessity if I was going to heal and be of any assistance in helping others heal as well. I turned my journey inward and as a result, I have gradually healed both emotionally and physically.

I continue walking without pain and am so very grateful for the assistance from my family, friends, and healers who have touched my life along the way.

– Jane Snider Shipley

Nobody wants to be sick. We want the pain to go away with as little distress as possible. Even if we can make that happen, in and of itself, this doesn't define healing. Moving beyond the primary relief of symptoms, authentic healing requires us to address the problem at its energetic roots. This involves more than just medical interventions, this means releasing the grief, fear, hurt, anger, and negativity that holds its correlative vibration inside of us at the level of *dis*-ease. The dense energetic matter of biographical ailments and negative emotions can work like a tuning fork, bringing the vibrational quality of our spirit to a consistently low level. Every weighted vibration or blockage in a body mass forces the flow of energy to alter its course like water around a diversion or behind a dam. Without the flow of healthy Qi, our body functions are compromised. We become vulnerable to sickness.

Like waves across water, vibrations follow vibrations. Like attracts like. So the longer or more energetic the vibrations of fear, deceit, grief, and anger embed in our cellular tissues, the more we will continue to create and recreate the same environment of fear, resentment, anger, deceit, and grief again and again.

It takes strong intention to raise low energetic frequency to a higher vibrational quality.

Each energetic frequency correlates with a specific level of consciousness and determinable human behaviors and perceptions about life, self, and God. Every level carries an attractor field that entrains (interacts) with the Collective Unconscious to call forth the manifestation of our beliefs and perceptions of reality.

The negative, destructive thoughts, ideas, and perceptions can keep individuals in a downward spiral. Sometimes these individuals are lost to their own Divine nature. Light. Love. Hope. Peace. These aspects only come as glimpses throughout life. They seem transient and distant. Individuals who live at this vibrational level, quite literally, need a savior: Christ, the Buddha, Krishna, Mother Theresa. The great teachers, rabbis, and saints—greatly known or barely heard of—have all vibrated at a level that can save the lost.

We, too, can develop that ability. When we live a life of a disciple, we align with the energy of Love. With the Savior. With the Divine. When neurons are trained to resonate at a specific frequency, that vibration elevates the cells, tissues, and microfields associated with that neuron or complex. The more neurons that fire together in this frequency, the greater the effect. With the right intention, the right vibration, and an elevated emotion, the mind will utilize the creative potential to alter, change, or affect matter. Whether as an individual or collectively in community, that energy resonates with a higher vibration of consciousness.

The energy of courage is powerful. Its strength is vibrating at the level where we are the source of our own life's experiences— where we stop taking Lifeforce energy from those around us, and instead, empower ourselves.

Most people have a resting vibration, not unlike a resting pulse. Throughout the day, we can oscillate up and down. Throughout our life or our lifetimes, we (ideally) elevate our levels of consciousness. We do this through prayer, meditation, conscious living. Reading from the great teachers and masters who have gone before us provides inspiration; choosing a mentor, a pastor, or master teacher provides guidance and honors the gift s/he can give. Quieting down to listen to the still small voice within as a direct connection to the Divine. Expressing unconditional love is complete surrender to the Will of the Divine.

When an individual seeks to transcend lower energy fields and levels of consciousness, they begin the healer's journey—bridging the perceived separation from Source. Sometimes it is a process that comes from an inner awakening, other times from a crisis. Sometimes the path seems completely indiscernible. Hawkins put it this way, "The readiness to initiate the journey cannot be forced nor can people be faulted if it has not occurred in them as yet. The level of consciousness has to have advanced to the stage where such an intention would be meaningful and attractive."[25]

Whatever the motivation, and however intentional we feel, the desire to evolve to higher levels of consciousness may prompt experiences more hellish than heavenly: the break of the ego or the dark night of the soul. As the poet Jon Berkley Wallace wrote, "We rise always by descent."[26] Sometimes that looks and feels like suffering. Other times, it's in the form of service as we humbly kneel before another. The opportunity to grow in wisdom is embedded in each dark and difficult event. **Enlightenment** is what brings us out of darkness.

In Figure 4.1, the process of Divine Intelligence manifesting in the journey of an individual life is depicted. At the dimension of spirit, we each evolve to greater individual consciousness until we are vibrating at a level of shared, **Unitive Consciousness.** We are all part of the holographic Universe. We are one.

Figure 4.1
Spirit: The Spiritual Imperative of Evolution

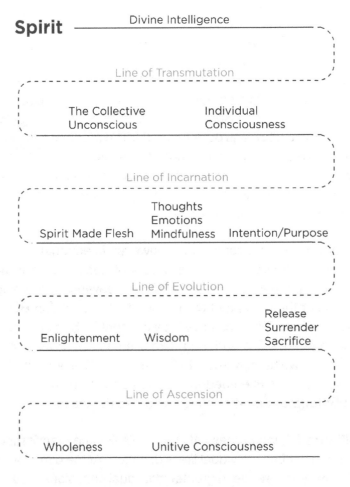

© Dr. Jill Strom, Cura Integrative

The healing journey is always a pathway back to our true essence—our true Divine nature. We are, like everything, truly spiritual. Regardless of the diagnosis, our healing journey will always be a spiritual one. As we move through the labyrinthine process, we will leave behind the weight of burdens that block our energy with each thing we release. In his book, *The Power of Now,* Eckhart Tolle describes **surrender** as "the simple but profound wisdom of yielding to rather than opposing the flow of life . . . to accept the present moment unconditionally. It is to relinquish inner resistance to what is."[27]

> **You always have two choices: resistance or surrender. Bondage or inner freedom from external conditions. Suffering or inner peace. Surrender does not transform what is, at least not directly. Surrender transforms you.**
>
> **– Eckhart Tolle**

While the spiritual journey to **wholeness** is an individual one, it is not finished until we align together in **Unitive Consciousness**. Understanding that we are all part of the same whole is Unitive Consciousness. To be *united* in consciousness is to have risen above self—to cross the **Line of Ascension** to the highest level of awareness that we are all parts of the whole. What happens to one, happens to all at the level of energy.

When you have crossed the Line of Ascension, you are thinking of the good of the whole. Not just what is good for you personally or good for your family or tribe, but for all . . . to the point of sacrifice, you serve the greater good for humankind.

Individuals who vibrate at this level are always found in service to others and to the earth, which is part of healing. Healing our communities and the world is the only way to complete the cycle that unites our best and highest collective thinking to the Universal Consciousness. We do this through relationships and engagement with friends, colleagues, church, spiritual groups or religious affiliations, advocacy efforts, community and/or civic organizations. And we must do this within our own families. We must do this first and foremost within ourselves. Joining our vibrations and resonating together produces the strength needed to face the crises of life that compel our individual growth and collective evolution.

Healing is impossible in loneliness; it is the opposite of loneliness.

Conviviality is healing. To be healed we must come with all the other creatures to the feast of Creation. – Wendell Berry

Unitive Consciousness means we are joined not only with humankind—but with all of which we are a part: the flora and fauna and energy of the Great Mother, our earth.

There is a Divine presence inside of you . . .

. . . a consciousness that moves in and through and around you. It is a Divine presence that also breathes and resides within me. Eventually, we will recognize one another. Mirror one another and we will realize the energy that moves through you . . . moves through me. We will awaken and remember who we truly are both individually and as a community. To do this we will take the journey inward and realize the Divine presence within. We will shed light on the shadows of our past, of our life story, of our woundedness. We will choose a higher vibration. A higher state of being. We will recognize our wholeness and, in turn, we will heal. We will realize that energy is transformative, ever-becoming. We will become from a state of love. Then we will awaken and see each other clearly. And we will be in the presence of the Divine.

Chapter Five

The Cura Convergence

**Happy is the man who has been able
to learn the cause of things.
- Virgil**

How close is medical science to discovering the cure for disease—starting with the common cold? Given what we know about the origins of disease, and the common cold in particular, we are as close—and as far—as we've ever been to finding the Cura.

Close in that medical science has advanced with such accuracy that diseases once sickening, disabling, or decimating entire populations have been virtually eliminated or treated with sanitation and medications that are effective and accessible.

Close in that certain problems or life-threatening issues can be addressed with genetic testing and stem cell treatment, or even resolved surgically while the baby is still in the womb.

Close in that cutting-edge technologies including non-invasive robotic radiosurgery, intraoperative CT imaging, proton-beam therapy, and telemedicine have created a complete sea-change in health care today.

Yet as far away as ever.

Far in that none of these advances will keep us from catching the common cold. Far in that this season's flu shot doesn't create immunity for the virus that is already mutating into the next strain.

Far in that bio-sciences and psycho-sciences don't collaborate and walk down the same corridor anymore.

Far in that the chaplains most often visit the rooms of the dying.

Far in that the laws of nature have established an important role for sickness as the catalyst for strengthening our immune system, among many other things.

Sickness belongs.

Sickness is part of normal life and serves an important purpose. Therefore, it's subject to natural laws. According to those laws, our bodies are designed to restore themselves to wellness. Our immune system works beautifully when it's working well, but compromises to its function are pandemic. Every day, we're exposed to countless threats to homeostasis from limitless external and internal sources—from the environment outside and inside ourselves. Each variable influences our Qi, and the flow of Qi directly affects every function of our body.

So while sickness is part of the human condition, our bodies aren't always functional for healing. We need interventions. As evidenced by the ever-increasing demand for more advanced technologies and better medicines, intervention is big business, and a critically important one. What modern medicine will accomplish over the next decade could be miraculous beyond imagination. Yet the cold will still be common, and the human condition will still include stress, anxiety, and a host of experiences that can manifest in *dis*-ease.

What hope can we have for the true Cura?

That's the question weighing on the mind of so many patients I see. After exhausting all other medical options and their own financial resources, they come to my practice as a last resort. They're hoping we can do something to ease the pain, stop the chronic sickness cycle, and, ultimately, make them well. They're searching for a Cura. They're ready to try something new—some different modality or technique they may have heard about. We can call integrative medicine "new" if that gives them hope, but in truth, its principles and practice are as ancient as they are cutting-edge.

Integrative medicine is writ in the natural laws of science and spirit.

Each dimension of being—body (embodiment), energy, and spirit—are connected in sickness and in health.

Energy, embodiment, and spiritual evolution are a lexicon for the natural laws of healing. The convergence of science with spirit happens automatically in the natural world. Each and every one of us possesses the power to create and co-create healing. The restoration of spirit is vital to the restoration of energy into matter. We can and must take responsibility for the effectiveness of that process by becoming more conscious and proactively engaged in it.

Cura—true healing—takes conscious intervention, integration, and grace.

Conscious in that we can choose healthier thoughts, relationships, and lifestyles. Our agency—the great cause-and-effect of our choices—can create the possibility and probability for healing. The consequences of our choices trigger the energetic response that, in turn, informs the physiological manifestation of that charge.

We must hold ourselves accountable to the choices we make, and alter the course that isn't conducive to our physical and emotional health.

Conscious intervention in that we can proactively choose the healing modalities and a treatment plan that can co-create healing. Eastern and Western approaches can be used in complementary support—one does not automatically preclude the other.

Integration of healing modalities in a holistic, dimensional manner that recognizes the holographic, inseparable relationship of energy, body, and spirit.

Plus Grace.

Grace in that the Divine imperative to evolve spiritually is the trajectory of all embodied energy. Again and again, the circumstances conducive (conductive) for growth are created from the raw material of our choices.

Grace is a kind of Divine goodness that reminds us we are loved by something greater than ourselves. Grace makes things happen for the good even when we haven't made good decisions. Grace is Divine intervention that redirects us when the path we're on isn't conducive or conductive to our physical and mental health.

The true Cura requires harmonic resonance of energy, body, and spirit to the vibrational pitch of wholeness.

The difference between treating and healing is that in the former, the context remains the same, whereas in the latter, the clinical response is elicited by a change of context so as to bring about an absolute removal of the cause of the condition rather than mere recovery from its symptoms. It's one thing to prescribe an anti-hypertensive medication for high blood pressure, it's quite another to expand the patient's context of life so that he stops being angry and repressive.
– David R. Hawkins, MD, PhD [28]

Do we heal from a level of matter, or do we heal from a level of energy? Do we determine the cause of disease to be physiological in nature, or vibrational/energetic? Are we a particle? Are we a wavelength?

The answer is always YES! Both/and! The answer is always the return to the origin . . . to the source: energy. All things are created first in and from energy, so genuine healing cannot be achieved unless the problem is dealt with at that level. A person may have remissions, or relief of symptoms, or transient breaks in illness, but unless the energetic pattern, blockage, or belief system is cleared, balanced, or released, the dysfunctional physiology, the illness, or the trauma will continue to be created or manifested on the physical plane because the energetic signature will continue to manifest the aberrant physical form.

Everything is energetic before it manifests physically.

Energy affects matter.

And the mind affects matter.

Your consciousness—the mind—is as important in homeostasis as the body. Your thoughts, where you focus your attention, your emotions, your perspective on life—they all influence the dynamics of your physiology. A thought can stimulate chemical reactions in the body that send signals, release hormones, and either alter the system to a mode of aberrant physiology or bring into balance the homeostasis of the body. In the ever-evolving dynamics of our lives, our consciousness is one of the variables that influences homeostasis—for better or for worse.

Dr. Joe Dispenza, in his book *Breaking the Habit of Being Yourself,* notes that the "analytical mind is the conscious mind, which is five percent of the total mind. This is the seat of logic and reasoning, which contributes to our will, our faith, our intentions, and our creative abilities. The subconscious mind, which makes up 95% of who we are, consists of those positive and negative identifications and associations that give rise to habits and behaviors."[29]

The mental corollary works in a similar way—much of what we think and feel is being processed somewhere below the surface of our consciousness. Our experience, education, and/or the programming of our childhood interprets and attaches meaning to our experiences. We behave accordingly. What we think affects what we do. What we continuously do becomes who we are. The more we think certain thoughts, the more we habituate certain behaviors until they are "hard-wired" in our beliefs and our sense of reality.

In the realm of neurobiology, neurons that fire together, wire together. So the more we think certain thoughts—good or bad—the more we engrave those patterns, mentalizations, belief systems, and reactions into our state of being. Those programs or mental constructs are reinforced the more we think about or hold onto the past experiences. The more those experiences are recreated in our lives, the more they imbue us with an outlook on life.

Learning how to control the mind—to become the thinker as opposed to the reactor to unconscious thoughts—allows us to heal old wounds. This self-awareness allows us to utilize what might possibly be our greatest potential for healing within and around us—the power we each possess to recalibrate our trajectory away from sickness. The mind has the ability to move into energy; to raise our vibrational thoughts from wavelength into matter.

All stories have a beginning . . . a creation. In holistic terms, creation is the level of energy before it is transformed by internal and external experiences into something tangible, palpable, and, ultimately, biological. As a healer, I enter the story well in progress at that level—where it has already manifested physically in my patient; where other doctors have been treating its biological/physiological symptoms for some time.

In the process of helping my patients heal, I have witnessed many miraculous things that we would all ascribe to spiritual growth and divine blessings. This, too, is Grace. This is a higher level of consciousness that is constantly and continuously engaged in what is happening at the levels of both energy and physiology. The Divine is omnipresent even if we aren't always tuned into it or inclined towards religion or belief systems at that level of consciousness. Divine Grace is omnipresent.

**Bidden or unbidden, God is present -
Desiderius Erasmus**

The hierarchy of our homeostasis starts at the beginning: creation. First is formless energy, next is what manifests into the physical form as created by whatever acts upon that energy; enveloping it all is spirit. Energy, embodiment, and spirituality are acting, interacting, and reacting in the present moment as well as the past and future. They exist in linear, chronological realities as well as nonlinear possibilities. It's a complex structure that must be understood in the context of Quantum physics.

I illustrate this dynamic to my patients to show that healing requires conscious attention and intervention to all three dimensions—body, energy, and spirit—across the spectrum of being. This illustration of the *Cura Healing Convergence* **(Figure 5.1)** shows the multidimensional interconnectedness of our physical, emotional, and spiritual well-being in the matrix of energy, our Lifeforce.

Figure 5.1 Cura Healing Convergence©

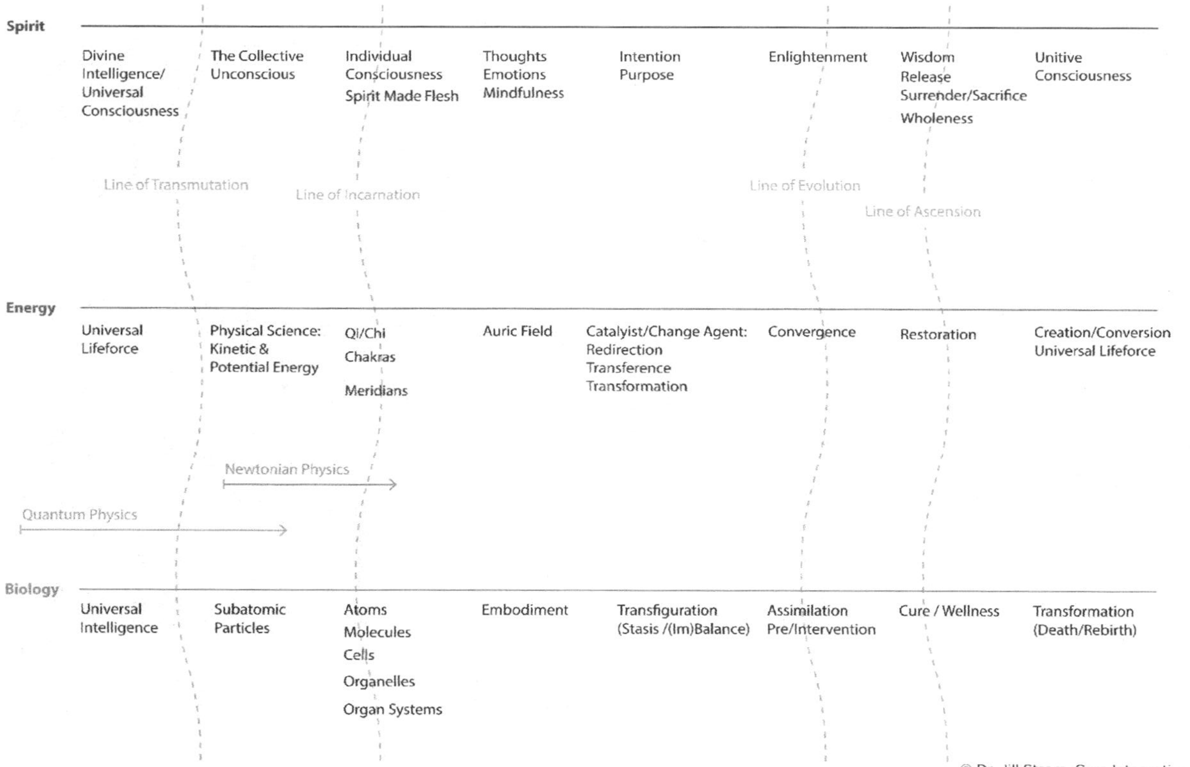

Spirit

| Divine Intelligence/ Universal Consciousness | The Collective Unconscious | Individual Consciousness Spirit Made Flesh | Thoughts Emotions Mindfulness | Intention Purpose | Enlightenment | Wisdom Release Surrender/Sacrifice Wholeness | Unitive Consciousness |

Line of Transmutation Line of Incarnation Line of Evolution Line of Ascension

Energy

| Universal Lifeforce | Physical Science: Kinetic & Potential Energy | Qi/Chi Chakras Meridians | Auric Field | Catalyst/Change Agent: Redirection Transference Transformation | Convergence | Restoration | Creation/Conversion Universal Lifeforce |

Newtonian Physics

Quantum Physics

Biology

| Universal Intelligence | Subatomic Particles | Atoms Molecules Cells Organelles Organ Systems | Embodiment | Transfiguration (Stasis /(Im)Balance) | Assimilation Pre/Intervention | Cure / Wellness | Transformation (Death/Rebirth) |

© Dr. Jill Strom, Cura Integrative

Our Body is the Embodiment of energy into our known, physical existence. This is the level where the quantum probability of existence crosses the Line of Transmutation to manifest into matter. From waves come particles; from particles come matter and elements; from quantum physics into physical science comes the formlessness that takes form at the Line of Incarnation: the body. Energy becomes embodied at incarnation, and life is now a being. When prompted by a catalyst for growth, the Line of Evolution is crossed and the body changes according to the variables and raw materials of our being-ness. Whether that change is triggered by normal development or physical or emotional trauma, there is either assimilation or intervention (Divine, medical, etc.) or both. This cycle continues throughout life until the Line of Ascension is crossed literally, although it may be crossed many times symbolically up until the point of Transformation: the end and the next beginning. Death and regeneration of life that follows all things beyond the Line of Ascension, whether symbolic or literal.

Energy is the foundational essence and the structural support throughout this matrix, permeating and manifesting at every level from formlessness into embodiment—the Spirit made Flesh. It is the intrinsic essence of this divine, universal life force that allows the collective consciousness to experience ourselves in this third dimension of space and time. To witness, consciously, the manifestation of I AM individually and collectively. The Spirit made Flesh here and now. From its quantum source in Universal Lifeforce, it crosses the Line of Transmutation into the realm of physical, Newtonian Science as kinetic or potential energy. It evolves, because evolution is the Spiritual Imperative; it crosses the Line of Incarnation, creating the Qi Lifeforce and Chakras system that enlivens our individual bodies. Whenever prompted by physical or spiritual growth, the Line of Evolution is crossed, converting energy one of three ways: Transference, Transformation, or Redirection. In its new form, energy integrates and creates matter from the variables of our diet, lifestyle, genetics, epigenetics, thoughts, beliefs, and environment: the sum total of probabilities and choices. All energy cyclically generates and regenerates each individual and all that comprises the Universal Lifeforce.

Your **Spirit** is an expression of Universal Consciousness that joins the Collective Unconscious at the Line of Transmutation. It evolves into an individual consciousness at the Line of Incarnation, and will continue to evolve uniquely as long as its energy is embodied, which happens at the Line of Incarnation. It is Divinely influenced; it is Divine. A growing awareness of this Divine influence creates ever expanding opportunities for healing when prompted by physical and/or spiritual growth at the Line of Evolution. Greater consciousness and enlightenment are always the purpose of growth, but not necessarily the outcome if we refuse the opportunity to evolve. The battle between holding on and letting go characterizes the personality (that wants control) versus the spirit (that sacrifices and releases to the will of the Divine) as spiritual evolution compels all individual experience towards wholeness. At the Line of Ascension, the spirit in its wholeness joins the Unitive Consciousness of the Divine. In unity, there is complete love.

Throughout life, we experience the continuum from birth to death in literal and symbolic ways. The purpose of birth is life as expressed by a uniquely embodied spirit striving to become whole as an individual. In so doing, this life contributes to humanity as a whole. Each individual life has a calling to raise the consciousness (and vibration) of the whole by doing so as a part, holographically.

The result of endings, including death (literal or symbolic), is always Transformation, both from scientific and spiritual perspectives. If life ends either literally or symbolically, it is the completion of a cycle. It is also the point followed by a beginning.

We can get excited about beginnings, usually, but the endings are often difficult. The endings can bring suffering and grief, but so, too, can beginnings. Starting something is hard work. It changes us, and change is often met with resistance. We may be ecstatic about the birth of a child, but that baby's beginning marks the end of life as we knew it. If that baby is born with health problems or a disability, life as we knew it ends again. And if that baby's disease or disability leads to new medical discovery or efforts that result in a better quality of life for others suffering from disability, then the Line of Evolution has been crossed many times into many forms of intervention, assimilation, and ascension.

Joy and grief, happiness and sadness, elation and despair work in yin/yang fashion throughout life. In *When Things Fall Apart: Heartfelt Advice for Hard Times,* author Pema Chödrön wrote, "We think that the point is to pass the test or overcome the problem, but the truth is that things don't really get solved. They come together and they fall apart. Then they come together again and fall apart again. It's just like that. The healing comes from letting there be room for all of this to happen: room for grief, for relief, for misery, for joy."[30]

Seeing the *Cura Healing Convergence* as three parts of a whole is imperative. Medical and societal norms classify life on the physical or biological plane. Religion centers on the spiritual realm, and science holds energy in the silo of its own agenda. Very few incorporate the whole spectrum in its multidimensional entirety.

It is essential to the Cura to consider all levels of healing—to tap into the vibrational essence of the energy manifesting.

- To align the quality and flow of Qi in the body
- To quiet the mind and ease the emotional body
- To balance the chemical and hormonal centers that respond to the neurological and limbic firings
- To ease the body into parasympathetic neurological healing
- To nourish the body with the vitamins and minerals it needs to continue to manifest physically
- To strengthen the systems of the body to work in concert with one another and their environment
- To align the body with the spirit to manifest its best and highest

This is how to find the Cura.

When we look only at the physical, we can get lost in the loop of dust to dust. We can see the myopic forces of Newtonian Science in cause and effect without the greater, quantum vision of the Divine hand at play.

And if we only consider energy, we can get lost to the Cataphatic needs of the physical form that require nutrients, strength, and loving attention to its parts and the whole. To look only at the spiritual—separating our carnal existence from the Divine—we miss the messages from our body and its role in evolving metaphysical wisdom.

Integration cannot occur without respect, willingness, and openness of mind. We cannot access the many healing resources without broadening our understanding of the universe, of the body, and of the energies that comprise the tangible and intangible beings that we are.

Eastern and Western approaches to Energy, Embodiment, and Spiritual Evolution are all intimately and inextricably connected in healing. They are all integrated and permeated holographically. As individuals and as a society, we must open our minds to this conceptus in order to heal the division of science and spirit. This is how we heal ourselves . . . and each other.

This is how we heal the world.

Chapter Six

The Healing Principles

**If you desire healing,
let yourself fall ill
let yourself fall ill
- Rumi**

The 13th century poet Rumi articulated the profound paradox of true healing: we are active participants in the process—knowingly or not—even before the inception of illness. Indeed, true healing may require a descent into *dis*-ease in order for us to confront or release something that no longer serves or supports our wellness.

The Cura Healing Convergence is a complex dynamic. When we approach healing holistically, there is no halfway. No short cut. True healing takes a commitment to awareness of our wholeness and what it will take to integrate energy, body, and spirit in creating a different reality. True healing requires personal accountability and responsibility for our own health and wellness. We begin to recognize the connections between the creative role of energy to its physical manifestation and how that is influenced by the collective conscious and Divine higher powers.

True healing can take us into the back passages of memory to places we didn't want to visit the first time (or second or third or hundredth time). It takes courage and commitment to the process. It takes a willingness to go wherever it leads.

It takes trust—trust in the process itself.

1. Healing is a journey toward a destination that is often unknown until you've arrived. It may be the cure you were looking for, or it may an experience you didn't know was the true goal, or it could be the transformation you didn't know was possible. However different this process looks for each individual, there are intrinsic, universal healing principles that remain constant: a) The body is designed to heal itself. b) The body is self-healing and self-regulating.

The philosophies that originated Osteopathy, Chiropractic, and Naturopathy all reference the vital capacity inherent in the body to maintain balance and innately direct healing. The miracle of our immune system serves to remind us that the body wants to be well and has generative ability to restore itself to wellness.

According to Hippocrates, "Disease (is) not an entity, but a fluctuating condition in the patient's body, a battle between the substance of disease and the natural self-healing tendency of the body." Disease is not necessarily a specific entity or condition, but rather an aberrant physiology that is attempting to maintain balance and restore homeostasis. In Chinese medicine, disease is "defined as the struggle between human capability to resist disease and the pathogenic factors. Therefore, many treatments are designed to motivate this capability—once it is motivated, some diseases can be cured easily," according to Dr. Xie of Beijing Medical University.[31]

The human body is always working to maintain a state of balanced function.

2. The Mind is the creative conduit of matter. As Dr. James Oschman wrote, "Max Planck long ago saw 'mind' at a finer level: We must assume behind this force (in the atom) the existence of a conscious and intelligent mind. This mind is the matrix of all matter."[32]

The mind is the energetic consciousness of an individual Life. It has effect on and creative potential over the organized matter that makes up you. The mind is also the creative force that initiates, allows, and aids in healing. Dr. Joe Dispenza states that, "You are powerful enough to influence matter because at the most elementary level, you are energy with a consciousness. You are mindful matter."[33]

3. Everything exists energetically before it manifests physically. Therefore, once disease manifests on the physical plane, you must treat it at the level it is manifest and address the causative vibration in the creative process that led up to it energetically, biologically, and spiritually. You must follow the energy of that creative process to understand the true cause and facilitate healing.

All things are created first in and from energy, so genuine healing cannot be achieved unless the problem is dealt with at that level where it was created. A person may have remissions, or relief of symptoms, or transient breaks in illness, but unless the energetic cause, pattern, blockage, or belief system is cleared, balanced, or released, the aberrant physiology, the illness, or the trauma will continue to be created or manifested in the physical plane.

4. Healing requires changes in behavior to break out of the cycle of *dis*-ease. As the saying goes, if you keep doing what you're doing, you'll keep getting what you're getting. Physiologically, that translates to neurons that fire together, wire together. Whether triggered by intrinsic or extrinsic thought impulses, emotions, feelings, behaviors, experiences, or vibrations, the patterns of our thinking and doing reinforce the energy created in each impulse, thought, emotion, feeling, behavior, experience and the resulting vibration. The energy and its route through the meridians of the body remains the same unless it is consciously changed or intervention occurs.

On multiple levels, changes in our daily habits, thoughts and self-talk, changes in our mindfulness, changes in our food choices and how we take care of our body all direct or redirect the energy accordingly. Changes in our environment, including interpersonal dynamics, dietary changes, and professional stress, will create a different energy and subsequent vibration.

One of my patients suffers from chronic health problems, but continues to give all her energy to a codependent relationship with her husband. Unless she changes her responses to that dynamic, she is not going to heal. On a daily basis, I encounter people who want to heal but don't because they can't achieve the change necessary. Their behavior continues to support the pathological dynamic that created disease, and for reasons they aren't conscious of, they keep making the same unhealthy choices.

> **Perhaps becoming healthy in some way threatens you more than you realize. Perhaps you are unable to let go of something from the past, or perhaps becoming healthy would alter the balance of power between you and another person. – Caroline Myss**

Things that keep us from making those behavioral changes are usually based in fear—we are afraid of what it would mean to change—of what it would require. We're afraid of the unknown even if it is creating pathology because the known is better than the unknown.

5. Scientific laws apply. Universal and Physical Laws that govern how energy works and why are valid—both distinctly and simultaneously. Quantum Physics applies to energy. Newtonian Science applies to the presence of matter and form. If the convergence of mind, body, and spirit is more wavelength than particle at a specific time and place, Quantum Laws will always trump Newtonian Science. Likewise, if matter is denser than wavelength, Newtonian Laws will most likely apply to affect matter.

6. Healing is not isolated. The experience of transformation and healing is both inward and outward. While one person's healing doesn't depend on another's, we can and do, in various ways, facilitate (or inhibit) the healing process in another. Intentional healing always maintains the focus on oneself— none of us is responsible for another's healing. "Healing requires that our life force be redirected back to our own life," writes Caroline Myss.[34]

Forgiveness is a step in the healing process. But the acceptance of that forgiveness and/or the reciprocation of forgiveness does not determine, hinder, or block the healing that is possible for the individual offering forgiveness. When we do our own healing work, it is always for our own reasons and personal growth. By grand design, the healing we do for ourselves changes our vibrational frequency which will have an effect on those around us.

7. Healing is reciprocal. When healing happens, there is a ripple effect that alters the energy of each individual in that relationship, whether that be between the healer and the person being healed; the parent and the child; between family members; between professionals in the work environment; or across friendships. That effect will influence the energetic pattern of the individuals in that dynamic whether it's an interpersonal or familial dynamic or the dynamics of a place or space.

In *The Spontaneous Healing of Belief,* Gregg Braden writes, "It can take one individual in a family to change what common science would call a genetic predisposition."[35] Ultimately, it is the power of love that heals. The source of that love is collective. At the level of energy, we are not separate.

8. The healing process is not just about construction, it also includes destruction. Like breaking a bone that wasn't set right in order for it to heal properly, the capacity to heal begins with the right conditions under which healing can take place. Whatever coping mechanisms produced a "limp" that got us around, however imperfectly, will not work in the long run. Life will re-break us—not to be cruel, but to create the opportunity to heal properly. Whatever construct isn't serving us must be deconstructed.

The universe works in creation and destruction. As the natural world shows us, constant creation, constant evolution, constant transformation, and then the decomposition of those states, are ever unfolding. A part of that process is breaking down or releasing that which no longer serves.

9. Surrender to the Divine is required in true healing. A Divine higher power (God or the Universe or Collective Unconsciousness or Unitive Consciousness—whatever name we use) is always working with our choices and circumstances to create the best and highest outcome. In that realm of spirit, Divine order encompasses the mystery of anything beyond our conscious awareness. Karmic relationships and "sacred contracts" directed by the Divine on the spiritual plane override the circumstances of the physical world. There may be a propensity to direct and control our own lives and destiny, but the point of acceptance and surrender is inevitable when divinely directed. We may or may not understand it or be conscious of it, but, ultimately, our acceptance of it prompts the understanding and, subsequently, the transformation, the restoration, and the assimilation to Unitive Consciousness.

10. Miracles can and do occur. Healing, remissions, and cures happen that are unexplainable to modern medicine. As St. Augustine put it, "Miracles happen, not in opposition to nature, but in opposition to what we know of nature."

Whether it is nature, prayerful-mindful nurture, or something our minds simply cannot yet comprehend, miracles remind us that we are participants in something much bigger than our own story. There is potential for the miraculous throughout the convergence of energy, biology, and spirituality. Miracles always happen on each dimension simultaneously. They are not random. They are not earned. They occur even if we don't recognize them, and their real identity is often mistaken. And the more we lean into the present moment and raise the vibration in our body, the more we touch the fabric of the miraculous. One person's miracle is experienced in a flash, while another's is only understood in hindsight after a long, labyrinthine slog through what didn't feel at all miraculous.

The labyrinth of healing can also be a miracle.

Chapter Seven

The Labyrinth of Healing

**Commit yourself to healing all the way
to the source of your pain.
This means turning inward and learning
the source of your wounds.
- Caroline Myss**

Lucy* was in an acute state of unrelenting panic. She was suffering from agoraphobia, anxiety, loss of appetite, depression, and intestinal distress. For 13 months, she hadn't slept without prescription sleeping pills that were only marginally effective. As she related these symptoms to me, explaining that this was how she felt for a period of nearly three years, Lucy was calm and reflective. "I was diagnosed with an acute panic and anxiety disorder, given anti-depressants and sleeping pills with a strong admonition to not go off my meds because the results could be dangerous."

Since drugs provided only brief, marginal relief, Lucy worried that she would never return to her normal life. "I had two little children and a job, but I really couldn't function. I would be storming around the house in a miserable rage at two in the morning, literally throwing dishes at the wall and wailing. I was in such despair, and raging—just raging at something or anything. My poor husband watched it all helplessly. I was canceling appointments with clients, and having increasingly dark, suicidal thoughts of not wanting to be here anymore,"

Lucy remembered. "I felt mentally ill. It was the worst thing that ever happened to me. That's saying a lot because I'd coped with many difficult things before, so I was not untested. I always tried to find the good in all of it, but I could find no good in this. None of the medical professionals seemed to believe a person could actually get better from mental illness. My doctor's goal was just to find the right level of pharma to keep me functional. But I wanted normal, I wanted happy, I wanted my life back!"

What was especially frustrating was that Lucy had been in and out of therapy for many years to heal from childhood sexual abuse. She had committed herself to not just surviving but thriving, and she was doing very well. Lucy confronted the perpetrator and expressed her anger. She dealt with each new manifestation that trauma had presented over time in her intense desire to heal and be released from the pain of those memories. "I really wanted to just get to the part where my experience could be made into something useful—I just wanted to be stronger because of it, not laid waste by it," Lucy explained. "There were many, many things I came to understand about myself from this experience. I learned to forgive because in my heart, I knew that was the key to my recovery and true healing. Honestly, I was genuinely thankful for the opportunity to learn true forgiveness. That was how I choose to view my history: to make a beautiful, useful thing out of this pain. And yet here it was, in spite of my best and highest intentions, this dark, demonic possession of my mind taking me to a whole new level of suffering worse than anything I'd felt before."

Lucy recalled clearly the night she stared at the darkness, unable to sleep in spite of prescription sleeping pills, biofeedback, and meditation. She told me she finally just gave up, or, more accurately, "gave in" to what was happening to her. "All the praying, all the talk-therapy, all the perfectly ordered higher-conscious decisions stemming from love, not fear, that I prayed would be just the right combination to unlock whatever dark horror was still inside me—I just gave up trying. I thought about the story in the Bible of the woman who put her finger on the hem of Jesus' garment. That was me, at last. Only the tip of my finger had the strength to do anything more. That finger was me yielding control of this process—to accept that I was down here for a reason. I decided to ask that darkness what it wanted from me. I felt it must have meaning and purpose. What was so horrible that I couldn't face it in my waking hours and had to be confronted at night when there were no distractions to keep me from looking right at it? What step had I unknowingly skipped in my 25-year process of pro-active, conscious healing?"

The answers started to come slowly to Lucy, but she found them on a descent into even darker places. Her symptoms became more complicated with tests showing what could possibly be cervical cancer. "How many times did I think 'the cure is worse than the disease?' Over the next year, I would learn that there was a step I had skipped. In my endeavor to just find the positive things that I could garner from years of molestation, I had successfully avoided dwelling on the fear, anger, and pain I knew as a little girl. I didn't know that 'her' feelings that had been denied expression so long were compartmentalized in real-time inside of me. Walling them off was how I coped with what was happening to me—I was just a little kid. It took years and years of work to get to a point in my healing process where my life was secure enough that I could confront those feelings of horror and helplessness that characterize Post Traumatic Stress Disorder (PTSD)."

It was time to face those "demons" if she wanted to heal. Lucy had feared that she was "blocked" in an arrested state of trauma—a message reinforced by medical professionals who view depression and anxiety as chemical imbalances to be medicated. Although Lucy took the antidepressants prescribed by her doctors, covering up the symptoms of her problem wasn't true healing and she knew it. Her doctors had not even considered PTSD, but an acupuncturist diagnosed it during the first visit.

Instead of accepting the condition as a life sentence, Lucy came to understand that PTSD was actually a sign that her life was finally stable enough to support the experience of opening up. She was ready to let go of those feelings that resided within her mind and cell memory. "My finger had actually been on the hem of a prayer all along, and this dark, horrible place I'd come to was not a dead-end but only part of the labyrinth of healing. I was still following the thread of spiritual guidance, but how could I recognize it in such a horrific form?" Lucy wondered.

**The soul always knows what to do to heal itself. The challenge is to silence the mind.
– Caroline Myss**

Lucy's healing had prepared her for the hardest part of the process: the trauma to her mind and body that resided in Lucy's cell tissue energetically and physiologically. Rather than take anti-depressants or ignore her condition, again, Lucy committed to true healing. A combination of acupuncture, Eye Motion Desensitization Reprogramming (EMDR) with a trained psychotherapist, talk therapy, meditation, and a supportive, close circle of family and friends who could be present with her through this phase worked together like midwives to birth the woman who would emerge fully integrated and healed.

"During that time, I was devouring books by Louise Hay, Neale Donald Walsh, Hannah Hurnard, and Caroline Myss. Each one gave me something new and helpful. Ironically, I had just received bad news from a biopsy when I came to the realization that everything happening to me was still about healing. I was healing from an entire childhood of sexual and sometimes physical abuse—even if it manifested as cervical cancer," Lucy recalled. "All the injured tissue and toxic energy of trauma was leaving my body. I thought, well, this is how it goes, literally *goes*—I'm going to get it out of me now, one way or another."

After the results of the biopsy came back, it took a month to get the next test scheduled, during which time Lucy experienced what seemed like a period that wouldn't end. She was worried that the test would have to be rescheduled, but for the most part, Lucy stopped worrying about the situation altogether. She told me that acceptance of whatever it would take for her body to heal had given her a profound sense of peace. She started sleeping normally again and felt more functional in work and at home. By the time she went in for the next biopsy, the bleeding had almost completely stopped. The test results showed no signs of any problems whatsoever and her doctor, albeit bewildered, gave her a clean bill of health.

"It was miraculous—that's how I felt about it. That I had to go through such suffering in order to truly heal—it felt exactly the opposite of what I thought healing would feel like. I thought it made you better, not worse," Lucy said. "From my own experience, I know that the process is harder than I could possibly comprehend. I would have gladly taken a pill if that would have actually worked, but it never really did. So my prayer was always that I would be healed, and eventually, I believed that I was healed even though my body seemed worse than ever. I knew the problems I was experiencing were signs of healing, although no doctor would have agreed with me on that. The Divine unfolding of my life, which I've shared in part and briefly here, opened the way for healing to happen because I chose it and I kept choosing it in spite of what it cost—my sanity, my health, my work. I just kept going even when I didn't know where I was going, until I did know. The path through the labyrinth takes you where you need to go in order to get to 'well'."

Today, Lucy no longer has a panic and anxiety disorder, PTSD, or mental illness. She has no gynecological issues or chronic health problems.

Lucy healed, completely.

Lucy has asked that her real name not be shared here.

When we or someone we love doesn't heal quickly or completely, or heal the way we want, how often do we conclude that healing won't happen? The idea that we didn't pray hard enough or that we somehow don't deserve to be cured, or that *dis*-ease is incurable are all fears perpetuated by our culture. A myopic view of healing is unintentionally reinforced by shortsighted medical interventions, imposed time-frames, and limited expectations.

Healing knows more about what its process requires of us than we do. There's not a formula for how hard to pray or praying often enough. There is no one "right" kind of prayer although what we create with our mindfulness (or lack thereof) definitely has a part in the process.

Thoughts are creative. If our thinking isn't affirming our healing and happiness, it may be working against the very thing we seek. A "beseeching" prayer (*God, I am not strong enough to handle this illness, please grant me healing from my disease…*) asking or begging for healing gives energy and life to the disease state or illness in contradiction to the affirmation of healing thoughts

(God, thank you for my healing and wholeness...). What you give your energy to gives it life, so it lives—and that opposes your prayer. Not only are your thoughts creating contradiction, but your behavior and limbic mind (emotional responses and feelings) are unwittingly working against the very wellness you are trying to create. Unintentionally, you continue in patterns that feed the sickness or disease you are praying against. It takes great awareness and intention to not get locked into this cycle.

Instead, be grateful that what you are praying for has already occurred. Give thanks for the healing that exists because of the creative energy of your prayer. Draw wellness to you vibrationally by setting your tone for wellness. Choose positive ways of looking at the situation as if your future—your healing—already exists.

Know that every choice, at its core, is motivated by one of two things: fear or love. Choosing the loving response is the path to higher ground. Love vibrates highest, bringing healing to our past and greater possibilities to our future. Love is the universal solvent. In its pure presence, fear-based thinking dissolves.

Remember that your body wants to heal—it is programmed to restore itself to stasis. The convergence of science and spirituality are divinely and cooperatively working towards this end all the time, in every way. Still, we can be "blocked" or at a point in the labyrinthian path healing often takes where there is no further progress to be made. A dead-end appears to have been reached.

What happens when you are at such a block or dead-end? You turn around, you try something you haven't tried before . . . you explore new avenues of thinking and being and doing. You find the next opening in the labyrinth and continue on until you have learned what you need to know.

There are navigational markers that will help you find your way as you move through the process of healing into wellness and wholeness. Pay attention to your dreams, to the signs and symbols, to the teachers who come. Practice mindfulness, knowing that these things are given to guide your path: The Universe is working in every moment and in every way to bring about balance on every dimension—physiological, energetic, and spiritual. This is true scientifically and spiritually. Events in life hold an energy that is palpable, vibrating at certain frequencies. The happy ones catch us up in a contagious sense of joy; the stressful or sad ones affect a heavier, denser mood.

When we find ourselves in difficult circumstances, it's important to recognize that we are at point of potential healing dimensionally. Everything we do in that present moment is constantly affecting our future and our past. What we do with that opportunity can balance the frequencies of the past circumstances that carry the same vibration.

What if healing doesn't make us better?

There is a common belief that true healing means the complete restoration of a healthy life: that the body clears of all disease and life returns to "normal."

While this is the case for many, this is not always the case when true healing is defined holistically. The underlying belief in traditional definitions of healing limits the context of our existence to the dimension of human form. The body in the realm of space and time is not the ultimate (or only) expression of our true existence. Holistic healing may require an individual to cross the Line of Ascension into Unitive Consciousness.

Our true essence is Spirit. We will always exist on that continuum and be restored to our wholeness in that realm. The expression of our essence is energetic and physical. Healing will bring us into alignment with our true essence and the fulfillment of our soul's purpose and sacred contracts.

Not all healing concludes in a restored physical presence. Sometimes life's contracts and purpose are complete; it is the end. Sometimes death is also a healing. Sometimes the contract is to hold the disease to clear it for the family, community, and/or the world. As Gregg Braden wrote, "All it takes is one person, however, in any generation to heal the limiting beliefs. In doing so, such an individual will have healed them not only for him- or herself, but also for countless generations to come."[36]

Forge ahead: It takes heat and pressure to make a diamond. Psychologist Carl Jung believed there was no coming to consciousness without pain, and that neurosis was a substitute for legitimate suffering. However unpopular it is to ennoble the role of suffering in today's Xanax® culture, it's critically important to state that sorrow and pain are harbingers of wisdom. Their lessons are many, including the ability to cope with difficult emotions, loss, grief, and so many other experiences that bend or break our hearts.

Learn how to suffer legitimately—without creating pain for others, without distracting yourself with so many varieties of addiction, without shutting down emotionally, and without imposing timelines on the process. Learn how to suffer so you will know how to survive, and how to help others through this dark and painful valley of human experience.

When circumstances are tragic, hopeless, or traumatic, healing may come with the wisdom that such experiences teach. The cycle of an individual life may end with his or her consciousness raised through suffering, sacrifice, acceptance, and release. Holocaust survivor Viktor Frankl believed "what never can be ruled out is the unavoidability of suffering. In accepting this challenge bravely, life has a meaning up to the last moment, and it retains this meaning literally to the end. In other words, life's meaning is an unconditional one, for it includes the potential meaning of unavoidable suffering."[37]

The true cure in the spiritual dimension may not result in physical healing. Sometimes the Cura is achieved in the Transformation that comes from death and leads to rebirth.

Discover your own path. Learn what is true for You. In each of us, the healing process is informed by the energy of our own formation—where and who we came from. Our subconscious is rippling with the effects of the collective community including our birth environment and people (or tribe). It is a fragment of the collective consciousness including our parents, family, church, town, nation, and nationality. All are embedded in our subconscious mind and conscious belief systems. From conception to three years of age, much of our belief systems is wired into our "limbic" system—our emotional responsiveness. This formative thinking constitutes the auto-focus of our outlook. If this focus is too limited or blocked, so too will our mind be closed to perspectives that could be important to our healing.

Live from the intelligence of your own heart. Consider that your perceptions may no longer be serving you. Open yourself to new possibilities and different ways of thinking. Commit to a meditation practice that can unlock you from habituated thinking and create space for different perspectives and new truths. If we cannot open to other truths, the Universe may well break down the barriers that are keeping us from seeing what we need in order to heal. That is the Crash of Consciousness.

Divine Will vs. My Will: The Crash of Consciousness

What happens when our subconscious and conscious contradict? A Crash of Consciousness breaks things the way collisions usually do, but this kind of breakdown may be critically important to your healing. Open yourself to it. What you perceive as truth is based on your level of consciousness or Ego, in the Jungian sense. As we heal, our Ego and spirit consciousness (as informed by Divine Will) are motivating both the direction of our thoughts and our choices. Their inevitable collision will de-construct (destruct) any construct that no longer serves the healing process of becoming whole, or that no longer serves our highest and best spiritual purpose. This is one of the most painful aspects of healing, and the root of much suffering. Growth comes from such destruction in the same way an island is formed by volcanic eruption. As poet and musician Leonard Cohen put it, "There is a crack in everything. That's how the light gets in."

Instinctively, we actively attempt to rebuild that which broke. It's frightening to lose the constructs that defined our sense of identity and place in the world. Quickly, we seek to create a new life that replicates what we've known for the comfort of the familiar. Don't. Don't rebuild out of fear. Don't rebuild to meet cultural expectations of what your life should look like. Don't even think of it as "rebuilding" but instead as an act of creation. What do you want to create?

Choose health every moment of every day. By choosing health, we choose healing. Many patients with chronic or returning disease want to know why they didn't stay better after they got better. Even as restoration and healing comes, life continues to happen. You can get comfortable with techniques and healing modalities, you can grow in consciousness, but other variables are at play. True healing is not just a snapshot in time. You may get a clean bill of health, then carry on with the life you had before. Wellness is a continuing, conscious effort to breath positively, to feed your body the right food, to get the right rest, to surround yourself with the right vibrations. It is remembering to constantly find center with your spirit and mental health. It is practicing emotional intelligence and self-love. It's a multidimensional experience of nurturing yourself literally and symbolically.

When life brings a situation to you that carries the same vibration or frequency of past, recognize it as an opportunity, a choice. Move forward in healing and love. This is the antidote to perpetuating the cycle of disease or destruction. Choose a different outcome.

Bring your best and highest to the present. Don't remain stuck in the past, dredging up your problems and pain story for anyone who will listen. We live in the present, so be present. Live knowing we can consciously and constantly create our future and heal our past.

Open yourself to the Divine Unfolding. Allow it to unfold. Allow yourself to transform. Allow the creative process and divine guidance to synchronize and formulate around you. Be an active participant in the design of your new life—but do not be the sole creator. That is not your job. Allow the Divine room to breathe life into and around you.

It will always exceed your expectations.

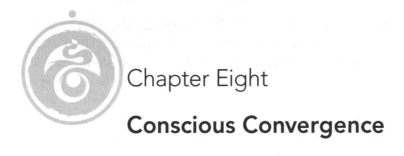

Chapter Eight

Conscious Convergence

You are ready.

You are living and being with a sense of purpose and intention toward your lifestyle, relationships, profession, health, and spirituality.

You are creating consciously . . . mindful of energy, body, and spirit in all that you do.

Then your best and highest intentions slam into the wall of reality: how do you live these values in a world that doesn't get it?

Really . . . how?

How do we heal decades of separation? Separation of Apophatic wisdom and Cataphatic knowledge. Separation of Eastern and Western medicine. Separation of mind and heart. Separation of science and spirit?

Moreover, how do we, as individuals, heal the separation of our perceived identity and true being? How can we help heal each other? How do we awaken ourselves to the dynamic, creative, loving consciousness within and around us?

In a holographic universe, we start by looking at ourselves. Each of us is part and all of us create the whole. To decide you are going to engage in true healing will affect those close to you; by extension, the reach to greater numbers is exponential.

So the starting point is You. Life spirals through the You who is composed of all your experiences from the point where You crossed the Line of Incarnation.

Chronological aging aside, life is not just a linear process. Healing the health issues you are facing today may involve going back to their energetic origins from your childhood. Western medicine can help us rebreak the bone and reset it properly, whereas Eastern medicine concerns itself with the energetic trauma of that experience that resides in the cell tissue even decades later. Healing modalities do not staunchly adhere to specific guidelines, and the Heisenberg Effect reminds us that each participant influences the outcome. Healing is cyclical, circular, labyrinthian, and reciprocal. Healing is dimensional. And true healing recognizes the contributions of all modalities to the real cure.

> **I honestly think that the right approach is a balanced one. You have to practice the best medicine that is proven by research. But I will also tell you that we are constantly learning and trying to be better, to understand more. I realize that there is still a lot we don't know, a lot that research can't ever prove. I also think that there is an emotional and spiritual component to this that I recognize but don't fully understand. I do think that the Eastern approach accounts for this better, and that's why we need balance in our approach. – Jeremy Strom, MD**

Regardless of the medical model or healing modality, each one of us will come (again and again) to a point of decision that commits us to a healing path—or dodges the issue because we don't want to change our attitude, behaviors, and lifestyle. Taking the path towards wellness can start with the next breath. Every breath is the next opportunity to change your mind and course—to recalibrate the conscious-trajectory towards your Cura.

In broad terms, consider your wellness overall by exploring the following questions:

- How healthy is your body, mind, spirit?
- What are your major health concerns—both physical and mental?
- When did you first experience them?
- Are you *maintaining* a disease state or *healing* a disease state?
- If there is a disease present in your body? Are you taking the right actions to best help yourself fully heal?

What beliefs and perceptions about you and your life have you been unconsciously agreeing to that you'd have to change in order to create this new state of being?
– Joe Dispenza

You are a co-creator in this life, and the owner of your own body. Your body—your temple—needs your attention and care. It needs you to draw your energy back to you in order to fully heal. Where will you retrieve it? What are you giving your energy to that is depleting the strength you need for healing?

Your health is a manifestation of energy, body, and spiritual dynamics. All of life's joys and tensions prompt energetic, physical, and spiritual response. Our health is very much a reflection of how we experience the sensory input from life: how consciously or unconsciously we process and attach meaning to our experiences. With that in mind, where do would you plot yourself along the Cura Continuum? Consider each dimension and the iconic experiences that affected and continue to influence you. The values and variables represented in the questions below are typical of major life themes. They correlate to specific dimensions on the continuum. As you read them, think of your responses in general terms.

Body: Your Energetic Embodiment in the Physical World

- Do you have any inherited medical conditions?
- Do you exercise regularly? Can you maintain energy and stamina throughout the day?
- Are you able to rest peacefully and uninterrupted at night?
- How is your diet? Do you have a healthy appetite for whole, fresh foods?
- Do your bowels eliminate completely, daily?
- Are you able to engage in your environment without undue allergies or sensitivities?
- Is your body able to restore itself to health quickly after illness or disease?
- Can you tell when your body is out of alignment or if you're injured?
- Do your bodily functions work optimally?
- Is your lifestyle (work, home, and extracurricular) conducive to wellness?
- Do you regularly spend time in natural settings—outdoors and in nature?
- Is your work or career satisfying?
- Is intimacy and sex enjoyable and satisfying or frustrating and unpleasant?

- Are (children, partners, family, friends, employees, colleagues, etc.) relying on you appropriately or dysfunctionally?
- Is your life mostly stressful or basically peaceful?

Energy: Your Source of Power

- Was your childhood nurturing and loving?
- Is the environment of your current home life enriching, playful, and peaceful?
- How often are you engaged in creativity? Is this often enough?
- Do you give yourself time to grieve losses?
- Do you feel a sense of balance in your life?
- Is there a good network of support around you personally? Professionally?
- Are the conditions of your world conducive to positivity?
- Are you short-tempered or patient, in general?
- Do you feel safe?
- Is the glass half-empty or half-full?

Spirit: Your Divine and Evolving Consciousness

- Are you supported in life?
- Do you feel seen and heard in life?
- Do you feel genuinely loved?
- Are you happy with your life story?
- Do you have a "tribe?" Do you have a sense of belonging?
- Is your lifestyle in harmony with your values?
- Do you take time for yourself regularly?
- Do you have a mentor, pastor, teacher, or group that you communicate with?
- Do you have a collective community that you are a part of?

- Do you participate with and within this group?
- Do you feel satisfied with your contribution to your family, your community, the world?
- Can you articulate your beliefs? Are they yours or adopted from your tribe?
- Do you release when it's time to let go?
- How easily do you forgive? Do you have regrets?
- Are you engaged in a spiritual practice?
- Have you ever changed your mind about something significant?
- How do you deal with pain and suffering?
- Is life sweet or bitter?

For Women:

- Are your cycles regular?
- Do you have recurring yeast infections or UTIs?
- Is sex enjoyable? If not, why?
- Have you ever or do you currently take birth control pills? How long have you taken them?
- Have you had any problem with conception or pregnancy?
- Have you experienced postpartum depression?
- Were you ever sexually abused or raped?
- Do you feel safe where you live?

How Thoughts Create Reality

The values and variables are unlimited. Obviously, these questions are not exhaustive of significant human experiences. The point of exploring them is to consider the issues and impact of each on your mental and physical health. In **Figure 8.1 The Embodiment of Energy** (below), the green spiral represents the track of each life experience from the point of entry—the energy of its happening.

Figure 8.1
How the Energy of Our Experiences Creates Us

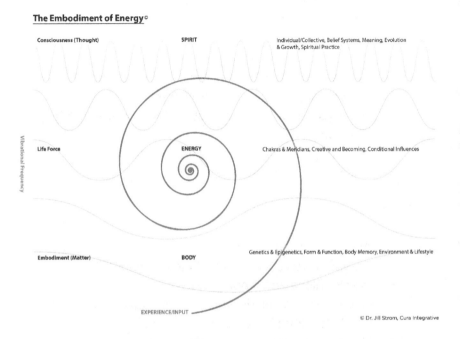

The Embodiment of Energy©

Consciousness (Thought) — SPIRIT — Individual/Collective, Belief Systems, Meaning, Evolution & Growth, Spiritual Practice

Vibrational Frequency

Life Force — ENERGY — Chakras & Meridians, Creative and Becoming, Conditional Influences

Embodiment (Matter) — BODY — Genetics & Epigenetics, Form & Function, Body Memory, Environment & Lifestyle

EXPERIENCE/INPUT

© Dr. Jill Strom, Cura Integrative

Energy—everything begins in energy. From the energetic charge of that experience (whether negative or positive) our **Body** reacts. We embody the event. It manifests biologically. It is part of us whether we are conscious of it or not. Because our Spirit/Individual Consciousness prompts us towards greater self-awareness, we are propelled towards evolving consciousness. Our self-awareness and reaction comes from the meaning we attach to the experience: "Wow, that was a delicious dinner" or "He hurt my feelings deeply" or "I never thought about it that way before." We attach meaning to the experience by processing it consciously. This is the level of **Spirit**. The process brings the growth (or refusal to grow) back to us energetically and the next cycle begins. All input and experiences—past and present—are cycling through this process constantly.

The meaning we attach to the experience is informed by our belief systems, our level of self-awareness, our community, and collective consciousness. Meanings may be those imposed upon us, or they may be the truths we come to through self-discovery. Evolved meaning is developed through learning Cataphatic and Apophatic truths and through spiritual practice.

This process spirals back into the embodiment (which is where it transmutes from formlessness to form because that's what "embodiment" is about) as we assimilate the meaning. We think and behave accordingly. What we have attached to attaches to us—for better or worse.

Our thoughts create our reality. As the frequency of energy slows from a thought form into matter, transformation occurs. This is embodiment—this is the wavelength of thought energy that manifests as matter according to the laws of Quantum Physics. **The Spiritual Imperative of Evolution** compels this process with each and every experience of our life.

In Figure 8.1, note the various wavelengths that occur at the levels of Body, Energy, and Spirit. Energetic wavelengths vary in terms of high and low frequency. High sinusoidal (curvy) waveforms equate to high vibration/energy. The more we move from energy into matter (embodiment), the longer the wavelength and the denser, slower the vibration.

The spiral above denotes the progression of our perceived life experience. It originates, for most individuals, through the body, spiraling into our Lifeforce, then up into our Consciousness, and back down into our body. Again and again. Our life experiences happen to and through us at every level of our being, altering us and influencing our Body/Energy/Spirit. In an endless and eternal cycle, we are affected by the vibrational pitch of the experience, and our unique, individual vibration is affecting the quality of that process. It affects the quality of vibrations we ourselves emit.

Now take a look at your own life and health—physical and mental. Go deeply into You.

- Are you whole? Are you hurting?
- Which aspect(s) of *You* and your life need attention?
- What attachments are you ready to release?

In **Figure 8.2 Integrative Healing Modalities**, consider the aspects of your body, energy, and spirit (in the left-hand column) and how they manifest on the physical plane (center column). Then review the Healing Modalities in the right column. There may be many dimensions and layers affected and needing attention. Help with priorities and clarity on your specific concerns are available from your healing practitioner and health care provider.

Figure 8.2 Integrative Healing Modalities © *Dr Jill Strom, Cura Integrative*

BODY	Physical Dimension	Healing Modalities
FORM	Musculoskeletal (bone, muscle, fascia)	Chiropractic, Craniosacral Therapy, Physical Therapy, Massage Therapy, Myofascial Release, Rolfing, Yoga, Exercise, Acupuncture,

FUNCTION	Nervous System Immune System Endocrine System Cardiovascular Respiratory Derma/Skin Digestive Blood Reproductive Musculoskeletal	Modalities vary greatly based on cause for disease or discomfort. Primary Care Physicians, Specialists, Internists, Osteopaths, Chiropractors, Naturopaths, Nutritionists, Nutritional Supplementation, Dietary Changes, Colonics Detoxifications and Cleanses Bioidentical Hormone Replacement

ENVIRONMENT	INTERNAL-Nutrition and Chemistry of the Body (Toxicity, Deficiency, Detoxification Pathways, Methylation, Heavy Metals, Minerals, Vitamins, Infections, Vaccinations, Hydration, etc.) EXTERNAL - Work, Stress, Pollution	Infrared Saunas, Footbaths, Chelation, Liver and Gallbladder Cleanses, Nutritional Support, Candida Cleanses, Immune support, Homeopathics, Ayurvedic, Vitamins and Mineral supplementation Meditation, Lifestyle changes, Counseling, Hypnotherapy, EMDR, Nutrition, Acupuncture, Feng Shui
GENETICS	DNA, Epigenome, Genetic lineage	Nutrition, Lifestyle changes, Meditation, Dietary Modifications, Acupuncture, Vibrational Therapy, Tai Chi, Qigong

ENERGY	Energetic Dimension	Healing Modalities
ENERGETIC FLOW	Chakras, Meridians	Acupuncture, Reiki, Vibrational Therapy, Biofeedback, Homeopathics, Nutrition, Tai Chi, Qigong
CONDITIONAL INFLUENCES	Internal & External Environments	Feng Shui, Grounding, Clearing, Crystals, Acupuncture, Vibrational Medicine,

SPIRIT	Spiritual Dimension	Healing Modalities
BELIEF SYSTEMS	Conscious and Unconscious Mind	Meditation, Hypnotherapy, EMDR, Acupuncture, Shamanic Journey, Prayer, Map of Consciousness
SPIRIT	Individual Soul	Meditation, Prayer, Akashic Records, Communion, Self Love
COLLECTIVE SOUL/ I AM	All are One	Community, Prayer, Transcendental Meditation, Love.

© Dr Jill Strom, Cura Integrative

Integrative Healing Modalities

Healing modalities include Western and Eastern approaches to medicine, but most of us are more familiar with traditional models. Western protocols typically follow **testing + diagnosis = interventions (pharmaceutical and/or surgical) and follow-up if needed**. There are many more resources that can be used in concert to aid in healing. The following is a partial list, and more information is always available at www. curaintegrative.com

Acupuncture is an ancient, natural therapeutic method involving the insertion of thin, disposable needles into specific points in the body to direct the flow of energy. It has been used worldwide to prevent and treat diseases for thousands of years. It produces no adverse side effects. Acupuncture treatment is effective, economical, safe, and simple. These noninvasive treatments can enhance immunity, support both physical and emotional health, and improve overall wellbeing. In the treatment of children, gentle acupressure is often used in place of needles. Acupuncture and other modalities of Chinese Medicine help bring the body into a balance and promote an optimal state of health.

Akashic Records provide us with clarity, direction, and healing. The Akasha "primary substance" is a dimension of consciousness that holds the vibrational records of all souls and their journeys. By accessing these records, you are able to more clearly see and feel your soul's intentions and desires. Although the Akasha includes all past, present, and future, the intention of an Akashic reading is to find and feel truth, healing, and clarity in present time. Within this soul wisdom you are empowered to move past old patterns, heal wounds, and find direction and courage to make choices and decisions that resonate with your higher self.

Biofeedback Instrumentation is the use of precise, instrumental, electronic monitoring of autonomic bodily functions in order to gather bioenergetic information. Science has shown us that your body is indeed electric, therefore the electrical reactivity of your body's responses to impedance, amperage, voltage, capacitance, inductance, and frequencies can be measured. The information is gathered through a universal electrophysiological biofeedback system that coordinates a complex electro-modal, biofeedback program with computer software. The data provides important information for diagnostics.

Chiropractic care focuses on the nervous system. Our nervous systems control and coordinate all of the functions of all of the systems of the body: respiratory, digestive, circulatory, etc. Any aspect of health can be impaired by nerve interference. Chiropractors check the spine for misalignment, or subluxation, that cause nerve interference. We look to the spine and cranial bones because they protect the spinal cord, which carries information from the body to the brain and back again. Subluxations impair the ability to transmit this information. Chiropractic adjustments help free these restrictions and help restore the nervous system, allowing the body to express a greater state of health. There are a number of highly effective adjusting approaches to help improve spinal biomechanics and reduce nervous system interference.

Counseling and Psychological Therapies emphasize guided discussion and personal sharing, for cognitive behavioral, solution-focused treatments for mood disorders, anxiety, grief, parenting, trauma, abuse, communication, and self-definition issues, among others. Mental health issues should be understood in the context of body, mind, spirit, and environment interrelationship.

Cranial Sacral Therapy is a method of evaluating and balancing the physiology and neurology of the body by releasing restrictions in the membranes and cerebrospinal fluid that surround and protect the brain and spinal cord. CST is a gentle technique that can be used for all ages. It allows the body to rest in a parasympathetic state to help aid in healing and restoration of proper homeostasis.

Hypnotherapy is a complementary therapy that "utilizes the power of positive suggestion to bring about subconscious change to our thoughts, feelings, and behavior" while safely and gently deepening the healing process. The light trance state of hypnosis allows you to quiet the conscious and sometimes stuck chatter of the mind. By quieting the busy mind, and then making positive and healing suggestions, this therapy can directly guide your subconscious mind to release old patterns, behaviors, fears, phobias, anxieties, and to even manage pain. Each hypnotherapy session uniquely addresses your current needs and desires, giving you the opportunity to make changes quickly and permanently.

Myofascial Release refers to a release of the muscle, fascia and the connective tissues of the body. Fascia is the fabric that binds our bodies together. It weaves throughout the body, as intricate as a cobweb in some areas and thick and fibrous in others. Tendons are examples of the thickest fascia in our bodies. The acupuncture meridians run through this fascia. Unwinding the fascia is a technique that applies soft touch to locate fascial restrictions and uses your own body movement to help release them.

Nutrition Counseling produces a personalized nutrition and supplementation plans for all ailments, including but not limited to weight control, diabetes, high blood pressure, and high cholesterol. These plans are designed to fix root problems, not just address symptoms.

Shamanic Healing is believed to be the most ancient form of healing on earth. Shamanism has been found in many indigenous cultures in North and South America, Australia, New Zealand, Central and Northern Asia, Eastern and Northern Europe, and Africa. The Apophatic and Cataphatic techniques used have withstood the test of time and are amazingly similar around the world despite geographic and cultural differences among those practicing shamanic healing.

Shamanism is a healing practice of working with the energy of pure consciousness to provide therapeutic alignment of mind, body, and spirit in this physical world. A shamanic practitioner reaches deepened states of consciousness in order to perceive and interact with the spirit world with intention to influence a desired physical outcome or manifestation, or provide insight and guidance for those requesting.

Music, Sound, and Vibration Therapies are bridges which connect the multidimensional realms to the 3D, and the intangible to the physical. Our bodily discomforts and dis-ease first originate in our etheric body before manifesting in the physical body, so vibration is a perfect tool, as it bypasses the mental body and supports a new degree of wholeness, vitality and connection.

Through various techniques, such as toning, tuning forks, singing bowls, and chimes, Sound and Vibration help clear and infuse light to your auric field, etheric body and physical body. It is a deeply soothing and profound treatment for anxiety, depression, Irritable Bowel Syndrome, thyroid imbalances, acute stomach pain, joint pain (knee & shoulder), Autism, and ADHD.

Yoga is an eight-limbed path teaching healing and integration of body, mind, and spirit through mindfulness, self-awareness, breathing, postures, withdrawal of the senses, focus, meditation, and unity. Ideal for stress and anxiety reduction, pain relief, clearing the body's energetic pathways, opening joints, lengthening spine, increasing strength, stability, and balance, and more.

All modalities work, but most of us find the ones that are the best fit to our energy signature. Using various approaches integratively from both Eastern and Western healing traditions can create an optimal environment for healing. Take the time to look at yourself fully, holistically. Integrate the healing modalities that best serve you. You may need different tools and modalities at different times in your healing/life.

Remember: while you may utilize a number of different practitioners and healers to assist you on your journey, you are ultimately your own healer. No one will know your journey as intimately as you.

Furthermore, there is no one more qualified than *You* for this work.

Chapter Nine

The Principles of You

**We begin to find and become ourselves when
we notice that we are already found . . .
already truly, wildly, messily, marvelously,
who we were born to be.
— Anne Lamott**

There is a part of you that is seeking, searching for the next step, the next cure. Wondering what you have been missing. Wondering how to heal further, deeper. Wondering how to become whole.

There is something within you that is ready for more. So you pick up this book. The *aha* moment, the next shift in consciousness, the mysterious thing that is calling you forward. You are ready to be present with and within yourself. You are ready to stand in awareness and reclaim your power.

The universal field, the collective consciousness, the vast expansiveness of dimension and possibility live within you. They breathe in you and are at your very fingertips. The consciousness within has enormous potential, creative ability, and power.

Therefore, once you truly understand your own power, you will realize that healing is ultimately in your hands . . . in your mind . . . in your choices. Choose wisely.

In all the world. In all of history—of time—of space—of quanta . . . there is only one you.

Here. Now.

So be present with the energy within you. With great knowledge comes great responsibility. You possess an ancient and wise and timeless spirit. You are the Divine becoming into being. You are made in the image of God. Energy and matter. Both/*and.*

You are the essence of the universe.

We have been shown by all world religions and traditions that the power is within you. There is a way to manifest love and wholeness and healing. There are as many ways to get there as there are people on the planet. We all have that opportunity and calling before us . . . each and every one of us.

We seek knowledge. We search for wisdom. For truth. And yet, the teacher that you seek is within you.

The healer's journey is not for the faint of heart. In essence, we are all on the healer's journey, the difference is in degrees.

You did not come this far only to come this far. The more you say "I can't do this anymore," the more the universe will conspire to show you that You are infinite, unbreakable, unconditional, and expansive.

Moreover, you always have more. Not more in the sense that you are not enough, but that you need to wake up to the Divine expression that is You which doesn't have limitations. There is always more to learn, more to give, more to release, more to accept. More to be. The Universe is evolving . . . always becoming . . . there is nothing stagnant about it. It is infinite. As are you.

So, therefore, you are always evolving and becoming, infinitely. That may be the most important principle of You: you are called to live every day of your life in the manner of all living things—to keep growing and becoming more You.

> If your purpose is to evolve;
> if your intention and prayer is for deeper, real, raw healing
> if your intention is to release all wounds, fears, and barriers;
> if your intention is to touch the Divine;
> if your intention is to understand the Oneness of all that is, then the labyrinth is for you.
> All you have to do is begin . . . and then begin again.

The convergence will continuously reveal itself to you in small ways: bits, pieces, quirks, wobbles, quanta . . . until you are ready to accept, assimilate, and exist as yourself wholly— energetically, biologically, and spiritually—within the unitive consciousness of the whole.

The following is a prayer to recite as you embark on deeper levels of healing:

> *Gracious Spirit.*
> *All that is eternal.*
> *All that is Love.*
> *All that is Light.*
>
> *I come before you.*
> *Surrendering my perceptions, beliefs, and will*
> *In order to seek the wisdom of the Sages*

And enter into the Peace that passes all understanding.
Asking for guidance, direction, and courage to know the Truth.
As it is revealed for my highest good and the highest good of everyone connected to me.

I give thanks,
For my life story. For the path that I have traveled.
For each soul that has come into my life to teach me more about love.
I release all judgements and blame
And I offer my forgiveness, to myself and to all others.
I extend my deepest gratitude for the choices that have come easily
And those that have come at a great price.
And I acknowledge that in the realm of Spirit,
Giving and receiving are one in the same.

I surrender the story; releasing all attachments,
And I welcome a new vision. A higher perspective.
I breathe in the Spirit of the One who connects us all.
Opening this temple to Divine Light.
Asking all that is not of my highest and best to be released.
And I consciously choose, in every moment, to embody the loving presence of the Creator.

And it is so.
Aho.

Chapter Ten

The End is the Next Beginning

We rise on stepping-stones of our own dead selves to higher things.
- Alfred Lord Tennyson, *paraphrased*

Dr. Jill's Story

It was in the wee hours of the morning. We were all exhausted but waiting for the last breath . . . or a miracle.

My mother stirred and called my name. I left the hard chill of the windowsill and crawled into the hospital bed with her. I carefully curled my arm round her head and cradled her. Her hand rested in mine.

"I'm right here," I said softly.

She squeezed my hand and gently fell back asleep.

"What profound love," Brad said.

I looked at my brother, puzzled, not understanding.

"Standing in the light, in the very presence of God, and she chose to come back one last time to be with you on your birthday . . . to show you her love."

And my tears fell like rain.

My mother and I share a birthday now.

Hers, to her eternal Being within the Unitive Consciousness.

Mine, to an awakened sense of self and purpose.

Reflecting back, I know that my perspective on treatments and healing are drastically different than what they were then. Yes, I still wonder. If I had encouraged integrative healing from the beginning, if mom was more accepting of Jeremy's position, if if if . . . but would she have even listened? She was so adamantly stubborn at times. And her walk was her walk—made right by the meaning she bestowed upon it.

I speak for our entire family on this. We wish we had more time with her. We wish we could still see her smile, hear her laughter, lose to her in cards. We wish we could still hear her speak on Sunday . . . still hear her cheer on her Denver Broncos.

Speaking for my brother and me, I wish there would have been a blend of Eastern and Western medicine working integratively to bridge the gap of healing. I wish she could have had *Both/And* modalities from the beginning. I wish the energetic, bodily, and spiritual truths could have informed the medical model that treated only an aspect of the manifestation of her disease. I wish she could have healed in a health care system that respected her life's journey—maintaining the context while removing aspects of the content.

How few of us—individuals or institutions—are willing to change or be changed?

My mother was drastically changed by her disease. I think she would tell us that she was, indeed, healed by it. In the end, she released (surrendered) all the structures and strictures that had confined her to the status quo that was no longer her Truth. As with all energy that changes, she transmuted, transferred, and transformed. Each step of that process was healing, even if her life in the physical sense ended.

With her end came many kinds of beginnings. There was a shift in our family . . . our own release of old structures. And a permission to claim our own journey—to call back our own energy within.

My mother still visits frequently. I am so aware of her energy in the sweet chimes that awaken with the wind, the wingspan of a hawk, the light reflecting through the stained glass at church. Her spirit is present. She is very much alive, whole and healed. And she remains ever so close.

– Dr. Jill Strom

To live with purpose, passion, principle.
To serve. To be able to always state
the reason of my hope . . .
to have my God say at the end of my days,
"Well done good and faithful servant."
– Joan Snider Strom Millard

Don't we all love the adrenaline-pumping anticipation at the start of a new thing?

New love. Birth. A great idea. Start-ups . . . openings of every kind that carry happy feelings of anticipation and possibility.

Once the excitement fades, a status quo sets in with a few highs and lows along the way. Life marks time with what has become normal. Good old dependable normalcy, and thank goodness for it because there are other beginnings, and just as many endings that need our attention—beginnings that may not be as joyful, and endings that may come as a relief.

Whether the end is a finish line, the end of the line, or the end of a life, closure is difficult. Even happy endings can be bittersweet, sometimes awkward, if not downright painful at times.

The end of life alters everyone involved. Lives are forever changed, even if the death was a beautiful expression of the natural order of life. Often times, death is sudden and unexpected. It's characterized as "before its time." Sometimes a traumatic disease strips away a person's dignity as it steals the future. Sometimes we get to say goodbye. Sometimes we don't. More often than not, we are not even ready to say goodbye and cannot handle the feelings that accompany such loss.

In Western culture, we have very few models for closure, especially on the individual level. This leaves a lot of open space emotionally when it comes to endings that aren't shared communally or marked by physical death. Beyond graduations and funerals, endings are rarely marked. Usually, we struggle with difficult emotions that are complicated by an innate inclination to hold on, so we leave things unclosed.

For days, weeks, and years, we move through our days unaware of the energy we continue to carry for what remains open and bleeding into other aspects of our life. We miss the connection between a current concern and a past issue that's infecting our perspective—usually unconsciously—because we haven't let it go. We never reached the end. In so doing, we missed the gift of closure: the emotional and physical freedom to begin again.

Closure brings a respect for the process.

Knowledge. Lessons.

Ideally, wisdom.

A greater or new perspective for the next becoming. The next level/state of being.

All things must cycle from their beginning to their ending. Without ending means exactly that: without ending. So, 25 years later, the alcoholic is still reveling in his glory days as high school quarterback every night at the bar while struggling with anger issues at his job during the day. The owner of a business can't bring himself to hand it over to his son even though his doctor insists that at 75 with his heart condition, the man is a ticking time bomb. A mother falls deeply into clinical depression after the last child leaves the nest, unable to respond even to her husband's loving support.

These typical human experiences have a common thread: no closure. Without ending things, there can be no genuine beginning of things. We can't truly start something anew from a position of *without ending*. The spiritual imperative to grow is in constant tension with the impedance of no ending. That tension begins to chafe energetically; it throws things out of balance and imbalance creates an internal environment conducive to disease.

What is important to remember is that the end is as necessary and, ultimately, as fulfilling as the beginning. Closure is just as important and valid, but it won't come unless the experience, the sacred contract, or the process that was begun has been fulfilled. The cycle of each unique event or experience must come full circle; it must be achieved before a new endeavor can be genuinely engaged. This isn't just a mindset—this is how convergence works.

All things begin energetically. So, too, in energy they will end— although not in the sense that the thing will cease to exist. All energy transitions at the end into something that is a beginning. Remember, energy can be altered only three ways: redirection, transference, and transformation. When energy transitions in accordance with the laws of science, closure happens naturally and the next beginning commences. Applying the laws of quantum physics, we begin to see that healthy endings produce strong beginnings when they are in harm energy's natural transitional function.

Closure makes a better beginning possible. Consider the ways energy naturally creates an ending and a beginning:

The guy at the bar leaves his youthful memories behind because he is finally ready to face life as the grown man he already is. This is *Redirection.*

The 75-year old man accepts aging gracefully and retires, leaving the business operations to his son. This is *Transference.*

The woman whose sole identity and sense of worth was mothering can leave that happy role behind and recreate herself anew. This is *Transformation.*

How do we become the kind of people who can achieve closure and transition effectively? There is no uniform answer to this very individual process, but all answers necessarily point to the personal responsibility each of us has to our evolving consciousness. As Frankl wrote, if we know the *why* of our suffering, we can endure the *how.*

1. Explore your fears and their power over you.

Fear is what prevents us from living the fullness of life. Some fear is healthy, some is dysfunctional. A process of introspection brings the hidden agenda of fear to light. What is motivating us—especially at the unconscious level—from achieving the closure we need? Fear of failure stops us from trying; fear of rejection by individuals or society holds us in relationships we recognize are not serving us well. Fear of heights might be about falling or because of a message internalized in childhood that we mustn't take risks. What are your fears and how do they show up in the choices you make?

Meditation, journaling, prayer, spending time in nature, dreamtime, sickness, or any experience that triggers a loaded emotional reaction are all keys to opening consciousness. Don't discount "coincidences" and gut feelings. Whether a solitary pursuit or facilitated by spiritual guides, a mentor, a professional therapist, and/or friends, whatever means we employ in self-discovery should be joined by healing modalities that address the influence of fear, stress, and anxiety on our physiology. Remember that the fear energy remains lodged in the cells until it is redirected, transferred, or transformed.

Internal fear can cloud perspective. It can keep our Lifeforce and our intention focused on worst-case scenarios. Since neurons that fire together wire together, fear constantly creates more and more fear. Illusions. Anxiety. Worry. Constant doubt. Never letting the body ease into rest and relaxation . . . keeping the body, the mind, and the spirit from healing.

> **A further sign of health is that we don't become undone by fear and trembling, but we take it as a message that it's time to stop struggling and look directly at what's threatening us. – Pema Chödrön [38]**

2. Make choices aligned to your best and highest.

In every moment, every choice welcomes heaven or hell, life or death—both symbolic and literal. In every present moment, in every vibrational resonance. In what we eat, what we listen to, what we think, what we open ourselves up to, what we surround ourselves with. In the relationships, the company of people, and in our environments, are choices that open us to health or disease.

There is always choice in life.

Choice brings so much responsibility. It takes so much awareness. Effort. Willpower and presence. It takes discernment between Spirit and Ego. Between love and fear. Between Truth and Falsehood.

Make yourself accountable to your truth. Commit yourself to beginning and ending consciously.

Stay conscious of reptilian brain responses that come from fear and emerge as fight, flight, or freeze actions. You are responsible for your choices even when they stem from instinct.

Choose because the choice is yours. Choose consciously because your choices create your health and your life. It is the hardest thing we will ever do and the simplest thing we can ever do: own our decisions.

3. Lovingly commit yourself to what you create.

See yourself as creator. See your creation as energy forming into matter. Something new with possibilities and probabilities has been brought into existence. It will have a life of seconds or centuries, and it may well have a life of its own beyond you.

If you struggle to complete what you've begun, it's time to introspect on fear. The opposite of fear is love. What is Love asking you to do for or about or with or through this creation?

The world we create externally is a reflection of the world we inhabit internally. Walls are walls, within and without. The road inward is just as important, if not more, than the road outward. So create all things knowing that they will carry the energetic vibration of their origin: You.

Do this lovingly. Be gentle with yourself. Do no harm to yourself or others, or to your creation.

Complete what you create even if the end is simply to let it go. What does closure look like for you? For it? Consciously consider this: how does this exchange and mingling of energy transition best between you and what you have created?

4. Surrender.

The mystical Buddhist tradition of sand painting, the *Dul-Tson-Kyil-Khor,* depicts their doctrine of divine detachment. Once the intricate mandala of colored sand is finished, it is ritually demolished. This symbolizes the transitory nature of things . . . the sacred process of genesis and exodus. It is a profoundly beautiful but poignant reminder that letting go of our creations is always part of this dynamic as a whole—the last part. It is the end.

When we can't let go, we are giving our power and permission to circumstances without ending. Without ending, we will bring the same energy-charge to the dynamic—recreating the same circumstances as we did before. The same life story. The same hurts or disease. Over and over again because the charge is still there, although possibly even more out of balance or intense. Release allows the energy to slowly swing back into balance. Allow this. Surrender.

We may be making our best effort to let go, feeling stronger and staying the course of our convictions. But the body holds memory and memory itself pulls us back if we indulge those thoughts. We fall back into our old patterns of behavior, take up addictions we once recovered from, and then wallow in self-pity or self-loathing at the regression. The perfectionist flogs himself with shame. The martyr never lets herself off the mat. The judgments we sentence ourselves to reinforce the negativity and keep us from starting again. They intensify the negative vibrational waves of lower level thinking: Shame. Guilt. Fear. Apathy.

Our own Divine consciousness remains present wherever we are in process. In the present moment of that love comes the wisdom that we are who we are meant to be even in the failed attempt to be more. Instead of a step backward, we've just stepped back into the river of change.

Dr. Joe Dispenza talks about the "River of Change." Once you dip your toes in, once you step into the river, the current changes you. You can cross the river or you can go back to the same shore line you started from. But the current will not take you back to the same place you started from. You will forever be changed. Even the shores of the river are constantly changing. And if you continue to cross, new life, new landscape will await you on the other side.

There is constantly a current in the river. It envelops us in newness. Again and again, it invites us to observe and love ourselves in all of those different states. It is about learning to feel our own internal divine guidance and hold space in a loving way for ourselves as much as we would others who are beloved to us. We often find it easier to give others the grace we need ourselves, but growing into who we are is about loving who we are.

So stay in your own space. Fall to your knees and feel your feelings. Breathe in your highest and best. Ask for help. Mourn your loss, even and especially if it is the loss of your own sense of yourself. Let that part of you be changed by the river. Let it float away. Let your feelings, your fears, your heartache, your pain come to the surface of your very being and be cleansed in the water of acceptance. Let go. Fully surrender.

Be gentle with yourself. Be kind. We are perfectly imperfect just as we are.

5. Mark the end.

The end of things is a natural process. The cycle of life happens according to natural laws that bring things to their end.

It can be a hug before two people part. It is the signing of papers to sell the house that sheltered you for years. It is crossing the stage in cap and gown. It can be the period on the last sentence of a dissertation, or a relationship that played out and is over.

It's the boy who left home and returned years later as a man. It's the girl who wasn't the same after she read her mother's diary. It is the miscarriage of a baby as well as the miscarriage of justice. It is the end of being the person who didn't know those facts and feelings.

It is that moment for all of us when we are no longer who we once knew ourselves to be.

It's the last breath, every kind of last breath, and the voluminous silence after it. It is the end in physical ways and in symbolic ways.

And all of this is natural. It just happens. Such is the flow of life.

Our job is to let the energetic charge ease.

Let it release. Say its name, put the meaning of it into words and mark it in private moment or with a ceremony surrounded by friends.

Consciously confront the feelings it brings. Face them. Don't just fight or flight or freeze. See the end, and know it as death whether real or metaphorical. Watch it. Observe and participate—not in reaction but in loving intention. Let the charge dissipate. Give it to Mother Earth to render the energy neutral . . . to decompose and balance it. To let it go fully. Release it to the Universal Lifeforce so it can be regenerated.

Let the cycle end so that what is created anew is fresh, clean, clear, and the natural process of becoming has a strong, vital chance to achieve its best and highest purpose.

6. Release the notion that an end means failure.

Everything that begins must come to an end. The end of the day . . . the end of a relationship. The end of a season . . . of a life.

Culture prompts us to do, have, succeed, accomplish while the natural order of the Universe is to be.

To allow. To accept. To respect. And to realize there is a greater power than us at work in this Universe.

We still should give our all and best effort. We should trust the Divine Unfolding of what was, is, and what will be.

7. "Live the Question" that can't be answered.

Destruction from an exploding volcano can mean the traumatic end of all life in its surroundings, but this is still in the natural order of things. There will be new growth—a beginning made possible by the volcano's destruction.

Unnatural endings are difficult to make sense of—they run counter to the flow of Lifeforce. The aberrant energy of such destruction needs to be proactively or reactively released. This prompts us to discover new approaches to healing because life has just propelled us into places where we can find no explanations that help us understand and assign meaning.

In its more destructive forms, this includes ending life without authority. In cases of murder or suicide, endings resist detachment and healthy closure because we cannot comprehend this ending. It runs counter to the natural order. When this comes into human dynamics, these endings don't feel like endings at all. They plague the mind in hopes of some kind of meaning that we can attach to them that would lead to acceptance and release.

Sometimes the meaning is a lesson in accepting what can never be understood. We have no choice but to "live the question," as the poet Rilke wrote, and "to keep growing, silently and earnestly, through your whole development; you couldn't disturb it any more violently than by looking outside and waiting for outside answers to questions that only your innermost feeling, in your quietest hour, can perhaps answer."

Sometimes the answer comes from learning how to suffer without doing harm in any way to anyone else.

8. Seek balance.

The next beginning is going to take you to the next level. It will change the status quo again until the next level or cycle becomes normed again. Then life throws it all out of balance so in rebalancing, you bring the new wisdom of that cycle into balance, expanding the sphere of your experience.

Balance works holographically: in each day and throughout all the stages of life, we move in and out of balance as we evolve to higher levels of consciousness. We are presented again and again with the opportunity to create balance and heal. Like tree rings, each experience is a cycle complete unto itself yet part of the overall growth of the tree.

When you wake up to yourself—more and more to yourself, your true nature—your world expands and the wider world expands, too. Your vibration raises and resonates across everyone with whom you connect.

9. Decide what closure means to you.

Closures bring wisdom. What do you know now that you didn't know before? Sit with that thought and let the ideas come through meditation, conversation, action, and creation. Name each answer closure and let them bring balance and reverence. Gleaning the wisdom of what was, creation can now evolve into something new . . . something becoming closer to the divine aspects of I AM. In so doing, matter returns to its original form: ashes to ashes. Dust to dust. Closures takes energy back into the void of the creative—the essence of possibility that exists in the Universal Lifeforce.

10. Receive the validation of science and the promise of spirit.

Life will begin again.

It will regenerate through Lifeforce, Universal Intelligence, and Universal Consciousness into new life as the cycle repeats from beginning to the next ending.

Trust.

> Remember, you possess an ancient and wise and timeless spirit.
> You are the Divine becoming . . . you are Being.

You are human. And you are made in the image of God.
Energy and matter: *both/and.*
You are the essence of the Universe.

And it is so.

Epilogue

The true path is the one from which you cannot deviate.

The stream was compelled by its destiny to reach the ocean. But the sand resisted, complaining that it was too far. The water called the clouds to help them. The wind and rain said they would do their part, too. Still, the sand was inconsolable. "If you go, we will change," cried the sand. "Whether I go or stay, I will change," the water replied. "As stream or rain or fog or snow, I will still be the water that must go to the ocean. And you will keep shifting to the end of time."
– A Sufi Legend

In endless cycles, all changes bring endings that contain the next beginning. The constancy of change is nothing new, but don't we struggle nevertheless with this most basic tenet of life?

Much of healing our bodies and our minds is a process of discovering the ways in which we have resisted change; how the people and things that have reached their end and need release continue to impact our equilibrium when we cannot let them go. As author David Foster Wallace put it, "Everything I've ever let go of has claw marks on it."

To not let go is to deny the true path. Holding on when it's time to release dams the energy that is ready to transform according to the scientific and spiritual imperatives to grow: evolution. Or, as Winston Churchill put it, "Change is the cost of survival."

While letting go is part of the natural order, the inclination to hold fast is surely rooted in our instinct for survival. Surely, we can be given a little grace for holding on to what is known, to what is comfortable and predictable. It seems preordained by homeostasis itself. But homeostasis—like balance in walking—is both altered and maintained by its process. Walking is easy until our feet outgrow our shoes. Then walking becomes painful. If we don't get bigger shoes, the pain can increase until, eventually, the toes and feet go numb as the constricted nerves start to die.

Here is truth: whether feet or feat, our physical and/or spiritual growth strains and ultimately breaks whatever is damming (damning) it.

In the process, the resulting tension threatens the *ease* of body and mind. Tension insists on change; tension imposes *dis*-ease when imbalance goes unaddressed. The body and mind suffer increasingly until, eventually, coping mechanisms are adopted to numb our feelings, or until we decide to engage in the hard work of healing.

Tension has an important role in the laws of nature, and, ironically, our homeostatic balance is subject to it. As we grow physically and evolve spiritually, tension's *im*balancing act compels us to regain balance—a new state of homeostasis that is reflective of the variables that influenced it. It's like doing reps to build muscle where the reps are experiences and the muscle is the wisdom gained. Yes, it can hurt to tear and damage muscle tissue, but that is how the body produces stronger, thicker muscle fiber—it is formed in the healing.

This is growth . . . this is evolution.

In the Divinely-ordered energetic, physiological, and spiritual convergence, tension works like fascia holding the variables of each dimension together. As a creative force, it is *both/and*: destructive/constructive. It produces earthquakes, floods, combustion, musical notes, and babies, among other things. In homeostasis, it triggers and is triggered by the growth of our bodies and minds.

> **Mental health is based on a certain degree of tension, the tension between what one has already achieved and what one still ought to accomplish, or the gap between what one is and what one should become.**
>
> **What man actually needs is not a tensionless state but rather the striving and struggling for a worthwhile goal, a freely chosen task. What he needs is not the discharge of tension at any cost but the call of a potential meaning waiting to be fulfilled by him.**
> **– Viktor Frankl**[39]

Without tension, we are rarely motivated to engage in the hard work of healing. The question is how much tension do we need before we decide to release . . . to let go? To surrender to the process that makes us uncomfortable or, well, *tense*?

Life answers by tightening the screws until we're left with only one exit: death or growth, which is, paradoxically, a *both/and* trajectory.

In growth, we leave behind what will no longer serve us in the next cycle of becoming, even if that is the person we knew ourselves to be. Leaving behind our identity is very much a kind of death. Dying to ourselves is, at the very least, confusing. It feels utterly contraindicated. The process can cause people to end their lives physically because they didn't know they could physically survive by letting go of what needed to die metaphorically. This is a profoundly, even traumatically painful process not unlike childbirth. In the natural order of things, childbirth—however excruciating—is actually about a beginning.

The wisdom of that most ubiquitous of experiences in which every single human being has a stake—giving birth—is surely to teach us the worth of suffering. Just like we develop immunity by getting sick, it is suffering itself teaches us how to survive the experience of suffering.

Learning how to suffer makes us more conscious of our own being and less focused on having a problem with what everyone else is doing. Things like egocentricity, jealousy, revenge, and cruelty drop their masks and reveal the vulnerable, insecure, and fearful faces we don't want to own nor let anyone else see. Suffering burns off the dross and reveals the true nature of our humanity. Whatever we are not seeing about our authentic self will be lost in such a fire or somewhere else along the path that leads us through the Valley of the Shadow.

> **Each of us must turn inward and destroy in himself all that he thinks he ought to destroy in others. – Etty Hillesum**

There is no skipping these steps, but don't we all grab for something to keep us from the downward spiral? Into the *noche oscura*—the dark night of the soul—as St. John of the Cross termed it, we claw at whatever comforts, distracts, or lessens the pain of dying to ourselves. When we are not the perfect mother, not the perfect father, not the model of honor and integrity, not the person everyone looks up to in this moment, not the guy who achieved the goals he set for himself, not the girl who would never *(fill in the blank)*, it's easier to cling to the story we tell ourselves than the truth we don't want to face.

Here is truth: You may be the person who screwed it all up; you may be the person who failed at the most important thing you ever tried to do; you might be the person who is ashamed of your choices, but you are still Divinely You—messy and messed up . . . imperfect but perfectly made for your life's purpose. Every failure is working the muscle of spiritual endurance if we allow it to alchemize into wisdom. Every ridiculous and regrettable thing you have done will cycle back into your line-up of options for the chance at a better outcome. It will. Try to recognize that when it shows up in the garb of another chance—an opportunity to give the best and highest you've got on that day.

Then trust the process. It will heal you medically, methodically, mysteriously, and/or miraculously with the kind of healing that is recognized as the Divine Unfolding of your life. However that looks and feels, bear in mind that it may be unrecognizable except in hindsight.

For You who strive to heal, there is no valley that doesn't rise back up the mountain. If you are still down in a valley, try cohabitating with suffering instead of fighting it. This is a form of surrender that opens the fist you've been clenching. It opens to the way back up.

This is the *enantiodromia*—the way down that is also the way up. This is the journey that changes you while never deviating from the true path. You are the journey and the path and the destination.

So take up your mat and start walking.

- Leeanne Seaver© 2016[40]

Author's Note

I acknowledge that this book is a collaboration of heart, of life experiences, of profound *aha* moments, of pain and sorrow. It was conceived from a deep, abiding Love that was instilled many moons ago, and it was birthed after appropriate time and space.

I give thanks for the many teachers in my life:

First and foremost, I would like to thank my family. Thank you for teaching me about loving service and constant dedication. Thank you for you always being equally willing to work and play. You all embody strength and are ardent in your pursuit to know and honor oneself. Always willing to see each person for their beautiful individuality. Thank you for teaching me that all are made in the image of God. And thank you for creating such loving space to grow and be nurtured in. We are all walking each other home.

For my tribe at Cura, my beloved sisters and brothers in Spirit, we have been woven together for lifetimes. Your very essence is alchemy to my soul. Same dust. Same star. Your songs and your drum beats will forever lead my soul back to Source. Thank you for creating and holding such sacred space for healing, expansion, and becoming. Integration can only happen as a team. We were chosen for each other, and I am so honored and humbled to work beside you.

I give thanks for my patients. Thank you for trusting me with your care and with your soul. Thank you for saying "yes" to true healing. Thank you for your courage and grit and vulnerability. You have all taught me so much.

Grandmother Dream Woman, the Traditions will carry on. The water will be poured. The elements, respected. The earth, honored. The Spirit, alive. Thank you for trusting me with such wisdom. I love you with no end.

Master Chen, my Healer. My Sage. The essence of the Universe lies in your very presence. My deepest gratitude for the reflection you give, the wisdom you impart, and the vibration you awaken. You are purity, humbleness and power. I bow, I bow, I bow.

I give thanks for the teachers I do not know personally, but who have impacted and influenced my life in dynamic ways:

For *A Course in Miracles*, for reminding me of who I AM.

For Marianne Williamson for *Return*(ing me) *to Love*.

For Dr. Bruce Lipton, Rob Bell, Dr. Alberto Villoldo.

For Dr. Caroline Myss, for awakening our family and teaching us a new language to speak our Truth.

For Dr Joe Dispenza, for guiding my meditations and harnessing my connection to the Divine.

For Dr. David Hawkins, for raising my vibration. I stepped into your auric field at a seminar in Sedona. I felt my vibration elevate as I got closer to you. And for the first time in my life, I was surrounded in and experiencing the peace that passes all understanding. Your essence enveloped me, your vibration altered me. Thank you for all of your teachings. And thank you for that vibrational signature that was locked into my cellular memory the moment I came into your presence.

And for those without whom this book would not have been formed:

Leeanne, my Muse. Words drop off your lips like sweet honey. Thank you for giving voice to the inner workings of my heart. For understanding what is left unsaid. For bringing your own wisdom to this message. For drawing out into the light this beautiful creative world that exists within me, within us all. For holding my hand, for holding the pen that writes the story of the Healer's Journey.

Joshua Van, I am so humbled by the purity and majesty of your Soul. You are the balance of divine masculine and feminine; your creative endeavors speak truth to that. There are no words, only tears. Drink them, and you will taste the immense love and honor I have for you.

It takes great strength, and audacity, to challenge the ideals of the world. Jane, you taught me how to walk in integrity. And to keep walking even when the world told you that you would never walk again. You taught me to honor the feminine power that exists; that was created in balance with the masculine energies of the world. You taught me how to laugh, to put voice to my truth, and relish in the simple pleasures of what matters most.

Finally, this book was written for my greatest teacher. The woman who taught me how to live, how to surrender, and how to be reborn . . . who instilled a great capacity of drive, resilience, and passion, and always reminded me that the Spiritual aspects of life, my relationship with my Creator, and my capacity to Love were what this life was all about: Joan Snider Strom Millard. I love you, Mom.

For all of these who have guided me and touched my heart, I bow to you. Aho.

About the Author

Jill Strom was raised in a family of healers including traditional Western medical doctoring, holistic alternative healing, counseling, and ministry. She received her undergraduate degree from Graceland University and her doctorate from Cleveland Chiropractic College of Kansas City. After graduating Summa Cum Laude, Dr. Strom continued her postgraduate education to become a pediatric specialist through the International Chiropractic Pediatric Association. She trained at Master Dong Chen's Acupuncture Institute as well as earning certifications through the Acupuncture Society of America, Cranio-Sacral Therapy, Dynamic Body Balancing, Herbal Therapy, and Nutritional Studies.

Through her pursuit of prenatal and pediatric chiropractic care, Dr. Strom discovered her passion of fertility support. She saw countless couples that had struggled or were struggling with fertility problems and knew that she was being led to help these people. She helps couples manage the physical and emotional causes of infertility and has helped hundreds of couples experience the miracle of childbirth and parenting even if they had been told that it was impossible.

Dr. Strom has a deep desire to help women achieve balance and health throughout the many transitions of their lives; be it learning to honor their cycle, preparation and support throughout the childbearing years, or easing into and out of menopause. She believes in the importance of a wellness lifestyle; balancing the energy centers of the body while incorporating chiropractic care, proper nutrition, and mind-body awareness.

Outside the office, Jill Strom loves spending time with her son Jacob, running, yoga, a good book, her dog Grace, her family, and wonderful friends.

Endnotes*

1   Moyers, Bill (1993), "Healing from Within." Interview with Jon Kabat-Zinn. *Healing and the Mind.* Doubleday. New York. p123.

2   Handel, Adam E; Ramagopalan, Sreeram V. (2010), "Is Lamarckian evolution relevant to medicine?" BMC Medical Genetics 11 (1): 73. doi:10.1186/1471-2350-11-73. PMC 2876149. PMID 20465829.

3   Mukherjee, Siddhartha (May 2016), "Same But Different." *The New Yorker* Magazine. p30.

4   Ibid. Mukherjee. p30.

5   Moyers, Bill (1993), "The Chemical Communicators." Interview with Candace Pert. *Healing and the Mind.* Doubleday. New York. p187.

6   Einstein, Albert (1949), *The World as I See It.* Philosophical Library. New York, NY.

7   Nelson, William (1982), Towards a Bio-Quantum Matrix. White Dove Healing Arts Ltd. Lafayette, Colorado. http://whitedovehealing. com/online-store/towards-a-bioquantum-matrix/

8   Walker, Jearl (2011), *Fundamentals of Physics.* 9th edition. John Wiley and Sons, Inc., Halliday and Resnick. p1105.

9   Rosenbloom, Bruce and Fred Kuttner (2011*), Quantum Enigma: Physics Encounters Consciousness* 2nd Edition, Oxford University Press.

10   Lipton, Bruce H. (2005), *The Biology of Belief: Unleashing the Power of Consciousness, Matter and Miracles.* Hay House Publishing. New York. p68.

11   Koestler, Arthur (1967), *The Ghost and the Machine.* Hutchinson & Co.

12   Hawking, Stephen (1983), *A Brief History of Time* is based on the scientific paper J. B. Hartle; S. W. Hawking, "Wave function of the Universe." Physical Review D.

13   Jablonka, Eva and Marion Lamb (1995), *Epigenetic Inheritance and Evolution - The Lamarckian Dimension.* Oxford University Press.

14   Hawkins, David R., MD PhD (2002), quoting D. Walter from *Applied Kinesiology.* Pueblo, Colorado: Systems DC. 1976, in *Power vs Force.* Hay House Publishing. New York. Chapter 1, p42.

15   Hecht, Eugene (2011), "How Einstein confirmed E0=mc2", *American Journal of Physics*, 79 (6). p591–600.

16   Lipton, Bruce H. (2005), *The Biology of Belief: Unleashing the Power of Consciousness, Matter and Miracles.* Hay House Publishing. New York. p68.

17   Childres, Doc and Howard Martin (1999), *The HeartMath Solution.* Harper-Collins. p33-34.

18   Ibid. Childres. p33-34.

19   Heisenberg, Werner (1949), *The Physical Principles of the Quantum Theory,* Dover Publications. p20.

20 Dickerson, R.E., and I. Geis (1976), *Chemistry, Matter, and the Universe*, W.A. Benjamin Inc.

21 Dispenza, Joe (2014), *The Placebo Effect: Making Your Mind Matter*, Hay House Publishing, New York.

22 Myss, Caroline (2003), *Sacred Contracts: Awakening Your Divine Spiritual Potential*, Harmony. USA. p3.

23 Hawkins, David R., MD, PhD (2004), *Beyond the Ordinary* web radio broadcast (https://www.youtube.com/watch?v=vA3gXjeFMl8&t=3007s), February 10, 2004

24 Hawkins, David R., MD, PhD (2003), *I: Reality and Subjectivity*, Veritas Publishing. p183.

25 Hawkins, David R., MD, PhD (2001), *The Eye of the I,* Veritas Publishing. p133.

26 Wallace, Jon B. (1981), *Looking for Home*, Darian, Ltd. Independence, Missouri. p52.

27 Tolle, Eckhart (2004), *The Power of Now*, New World Library.

28 Hawkins, David R., MD, PhD (2002), *Power vs Force*, Hay House, Inc., Carlsbad CA, Chapter 3. p73.

29 Dispenza, Joe (2013), *Breaking the Habit of Being Yourself*, Hay House, p15.

30 Chodron, Pema (2000), *When Things Fall Apart: Heartfelt Advice for Hard Times*, Shambhala Classics.

31 Moyers, Bill. (1993), "The Mystery of Chi." Interview with Dr. Xie, Beijing Medical University in *Healing and the Mind*. Doubleday, New York. p277.

32 Oschman, James L. (2000), *Energy Medicine - The Scientific Basis*, Churchill-Livingstone Harcourt Publishers, New York. p238.

33 Dispenza, Joe (2013), *Breaking the Habit of Being Yourself*, Hay House.

34 Myss, Caroline (1998), *Why People Don't Heal and How They Can*. Harmony. USA. p31.

35 Braden, Gregg (2009), *The Spontaneous Healing of Belief*. Hay House, New York. p105.

36 Ibid. Braden. p105.

37 Frankl, Viktor (5th Edition, 2006), *Man's Search for Meaning*. Beacon Press, Boston MA. p114.

38 Chodron, Pema (2000), *When Things Fall Apart: Heartfelt Advice for Hard Times*, Shambhala Classics.

39 Ibid. Frankl. p114.

40 Seaver, Leeanne (16 October 2016), *"Enantiodromia"* on www. Iwastoldtherewouldbenomath.wordpress.com, Wordpress, USA.

*The author cannot verify or assure any references to online sources whose publication may or may not be accessible due to circumstances beyond the control of Jill Strom or Cura Integrative.